Top Executive Compensation: 1991 Edition

by Elizabeth R. Arreglado

Contents

Tables

Charts

About the Author

Elizabeth R. Arreglado is Research Associate, Corporate Practices Program. She plans and conducts the Board's research on corporate compensation programs. Her most recent published reports are: *Corporate Directors' Compensation, 1991 Edition;* and *Top Executive Compensation: 1990 Edition.*

Author's Acknowledgment

Analytical programming was provided by William Dole. Charts were prepared by Chuck N. Tow, Chief Chartist. Charles Peck, Senior Research Associate, assisted with the interpretation of the data. Elizabeth Miranda, Junior Editor, assisted in editing the report.

From The President

The impact of the recession varied greatly according to industry. As a result, executive compensation, which is contingent upon business conditions, differed considerably among the industries surveyed.

The average 1990 total current compensation (salary and bonus) of the five highest paid executives in eight major industries is presented in this report. Long-term incentive arrangements, now an integral part of executive compensation, are reported on in some detail. These programs reward executives for company performance over time, thus linking the interests of the executives to the long-term prosperity of the corporation and, ultimately, the shareholders.

The report, designed for maximum clarity and ease of interpretation, will serve as a benchmark for determining competitive levels of executive compensation according to company size and type of industry. We thank the several hundred companies that provided the invaluable information necessary to make this report possible.

PRESTON TOWNLEY
President and CEO

Executive Summary

As this uncertain economy challenges companies to achieve profitability and competitiveness, it is increasingly urgent to retain and motivate valued executives. Based on a survey of 649 companies, the 1990 compensation of the five highest-paid executives in eight major types of businesses is examined. The major focus is on 1990 total current compensation, defined as base salary paid in 1990 plus bonus earned for 1990 company performance. This report enables the user to examine the diversity of executive compensation programs in companies of similar, as well as different, sizes and industries.

The report also describes the incidence of, and trends in, four important elements of the executive compensation package: annual bonus plans, long-term performance plans, stock option plans, and restricted stock plans. For stock options, the size of option grants during 1990 is shown, as well as the net gain for options exercised during 1990. For restricted stock plans, the size of grants during 1990 is reported. The size of payouts during 1990 is given for long-term performance plans, and the size of contingent awards made under these plans during the year is also reported.

Pay Trends

Compared with 1989, 1990 total current compensation (salary and bonus) rose in all the industries surveyed. The greatest increase was in the energy industry where total compensation increased by 16.1 percent.

Total current compensation increased by 9.1 percent in insurance; 8.9 percent in trade; 8.5 percent in diversified services; 6.4 percent in utilities; 2.7 percent in commercial banking; and 1.0 percent in manufacturing.

Salaries, likewise, rose in 1990 in each type of business. They increased 8.6 percent in insurance; 7.9 percent in trade; 7.5 percent in energy; 6.7 percent in manufacturing; 6.6 percent in utilities; 6.5 percent in diversified services; and 5.1 percent in commercial banking. There

was insufficient data to show a pay trend for communications.

Median CEO total current compensation was the highest in energy at $809,000. Median CEO compensation in the other seven industry sectors was: manufacturing, $730,000; diversified services, $666,000; communications, $630,000; insurance, $533,000; trade, $512,000; commercial banking, $470,000; and utilities, $458,000.

A survey of salary increase budgets for all salaried employees, also conducted in April and May 1991, shows median budgets of 5.0 percent for nonexempt, exempt and executives for 1990. This drop from the 5.5 percent projected by companies last year may have been the result of companies rethinking their 1991 plans in response to the recession. Projected 1992 salary increase budgets for all employee groups are expected to remain at 5.0 percent, which may indicate business' continued concern with controlling costs.

Annual Bonus Plans

Annual bonus plans are used by almost all companies in all industries except insurance and utilities; 85 percent of the insurance carriers and 86 percent of utilities reported such plans. These figures, however, show an increase of 25 percent and 79 percent respectively over numbers reported in 1986.

The median bonus award for the CEO, as a percentage of salary, is lowest in utilities and communications; 32 percent and 35 percent, respectively. Similar levels are reported for banking, 38 percent, and insurance, 40 percent. Manufacturing and trade paid a median bonus of 55 percent, while diversified services paid a median bonus of 58 percent. Energy was the highest payer, with a median CEO bonus of 64 percent.

Annual bonuses are driven by short-term profits. Thus, energy, where profits seemed to be the least affected by the economic downturn, paid the highest bonus.

Long-term Compensation Plans

Long-term incentive arrangements, such as restricted stock plans, long-term performance plans, and stock options, reward executives for business performance over a period of years thereby enhancing long-term growth.

Restricted Stock Plans

Under these plans, companies make outright awards of restricted shares, which are often subject to forfeiture until they are "earned out" over a stipulated period of continued employment. More plans awarding restricted stock to top executives were reported in 1990 in all industries except utilities, where only 23 percent reported them compared with 30 percent in 1989. The prevalence among the seven other industries is: energy companies, 54 percent; manufacturing, 46 percent; diversified services, 42 percent; banks, 41 percent; communications, 38 percent; trade, 31 percent; and stock insurance companies, 29 percent.

During 1990, the median award to the five highest-paid executives as a group ranged from a high of 81 percent of salary in diversified services and commercial banking, to a low of 23 percent in utilities.

Long-Term Performance Plans

A significant minority of companies in each industry group have long-term performance plans. Under these plans, top executives are given a contingent award of shares or units at the beginning of a performance period. The payment of these awards is determined by how closely corporate financial targets are met during a three-four- or five-year performance cycle. Such plans are most prevalent in communications (48 percent) and manufacturing (41 percent). Thirty-eight percent of the surveyed energy companies have long-term performance plans, as do 31 percent of the insurance companies. Long-term plans are found in 27 percent of the utilities and 24 percent of trade. They are least frequent in commercial banking (18 percent) and diversified services (20 percent).

During 1990, the median contingent *award* to the five highest-paid executives as a group ranged from 142 percent of salary in energy to 25 percent of salary in utilities. The median *payment* for 1990 ranged from 51 percent of salary among manufacturing companies to 23 percent among trade companies.

Stock Option Plans

The majority of companies in all industry categories have stock option plans. Ninety-five percent of the surveyed energy companies have them, as do 83 percent of the manufacturing companies; 81 percent of the communications companies; 78 percent of trade; 76 percent of the banks; 75 percent of the stock insurance companies; 68 percent of the diversified service companies; and 52 percent of the utilities.

The median stock option grant made in 1990 to the five highest-paid executives as a group ranged from the equivalent of 99 percent to 184 percent of base salary, depending on the type of business. The median net gain for options exercised during 1990 ranged from a high of 81 percent of salary in commercial banking, to a low of 53 percent in diversified services.

Method

Information for this report was collected during April and May 1991. Questionnaires were mailed to 2,721 U.S. companies. Those surveyed were medium to large manufacturers (sales of approximately $100 million or more) and companies of comparable size in seven other industry categories. The survey information was supplemented with publicly available data from corporate reports.

Usable information was collected from 649 companies in eight industry categories. The 649 companies were distributed by industry category as follows:

Manufacturing companies (300)

Health, life and property, and casualty insurance companies (67)

Commercial banks (66)

Utilities, including gas, electric, water and telecommunications (66)

Diversified service companies, including computer services, construction/design/engineering, health care, hotel/restaurant/ entertainment, real estate, and transportation (60)

Energy and natural resources companies (37)

Wholesale and retail trade companies (32)

Introduction

This report provides an analysis of the 1990 compensation of the five highest-paid executives in each of 649 companies (see Method box). The major emphasis is on base salary *paid* in 1990 and the bonus *earned* for 1990 company performance, regardless of when paid. Total current compensation is the sum of the two. The report also describes the prevalence of and trends in four major forms of executive incentive compensation: annual bonus plans, restricted stock plans, long-term performance plans, and stock option plans.

Pay Trends

The change in CEO total current compensation from 1989 to 1990 is given in Table 1 below. This is the median change for the *function* in those companies that

furnished data in both years. The *individuals* in the CEO function were not necessarily the same in both years. The same information with respect to salary is shown in Table 2.

As an indicator of future salary increases, companies were asked during April and May 1991 to provide the 1991 salary increase budget and the 1992 anticipated salary increase budget for their nonexempt, exempt and executive populations. The results are shown in Table 3 for all industries as a group and separately for those industries with sufficient data to allow individual analysis.

Table 1: CEO Total Current Compensation Change, 1990 over 1989

Industry Category*	Number of Companies	Median Change
Energy	19	16.1%
Insurance	45	9.1
Trade	17	8.9
Diversified services	36	8.5
Utilities	48	6.4
Commercial Banking	35	2.7
Manufacturing	129	1.0

Table 2: CEO Salary Change, 1990 over 1989

Industry Category*	Number of Companies	Median Change
Insurance	45	8.6%
Trade	17	7.9
Energy	19	7.5
Manufacturing	129	6.7
Utilities	48	6.6
Diversified services	36	6.5
Commercial Banking	35	5.1

*Insufficient data for Communications.

Table 3: Salary Increase Budgets, 1991 and 1992

(N=537)	1991		Estimated for 1992	
Type of Business	Number of Companies*	Median	Number of Companies*	Median
ALL INDUSTRIES				
Nonexempt	511	5.0%	369	5.0%
Exempt	518	5.0	374	5.0
Executive	479	5.0	352	5.0
COMMERCIAL BANKING				
Nonexempt	71	5.0	45	5.0
Exempt	69	5.0	44	5.0
Executive	64	4.8	41	5.0
DIVERSIFIED SERVICES				
Nonexempt	39	5.0	37	5.0
Exempt	40	5.4	38	5.0
Executive	37	5.1	35	5.0
INSURANCE				
Nonexempt	67	5.4	48	5.0
Exempt	68	5.5	47	5.0
Executive	67	5.5	47	5.0
MANUFACTURING				
Nonexempt	196	5.0	153	5.0
Exempt	198	5.0	155	5.0
Executive	182	5.0	145	5.0
TRADE				
Nonexempt	24	4.8	14	4.8
Exempt	25	5.0	15	5.0
Executive	24	5.0	15	5.0
UTILITIES				
Nonexempt	58	4.6	41	5.0
Exempt	62	5.0	44	5.0
Executive	59	5.4	42	5.4

* Other industry groups are included in totals but not shown separately because of small samples.

Executive Incentive Compensation

The four major forms of executive incentive compensation are:

Annual Bonus: Generally, a percentage of profits is used to create a fund that is apportioned among the eligible executives based on individual contributions to profitability.

Restricted Stock: Shares of company stock are awarded to executives and are subject to restrictions as to sale or transfer, usually for three to five years. Additional restrictions often call for forfeiture if the executive terminates employment during the restricted period.

Long-Term Performance Plans: Under these plans, executives are awarded contingent grants of cash (long-term performance units) or stock (long-term performance shares). The payment of the award usually depends upon the achievement of three- to five-year financial performance goals.

Stock Options: These arrangements provide executives with rights to purchase shares of company stock at a fixed price over a stated period of time. "Incentive stock options" (ISOs) meet Internal Revenue Code requirements, while "nonqualified stock options" do not. An option plan may allow "stock swaps" where previously acquired shares are used to exercise an option. "Stock appreciation rights" (SARs) may be attached to stock options. The SAR gives an optionee, in lieu of exercising the stock option in whole or in part, the right to receive an amount equal to the appreciation in the stock price since the date of grant.

A five-year span is believed to be a good indicator of the prevalence of these plans. Therefore, the number reported in the 1991 survey is compared with the number reported in the 1986 survey. It should be noted that while the companies in the two surveys are not identical, they remain relatively constant.

Table 4: Prevalence of Annual Bonus Plans

Industry Category		May, 1991		May, 1986
	Total Companies	With Bonus Plan Number	Percent	Percent With Bonus Plan
Energy	37	37	100%	*
Manufacturing	300	295	98	91%
Communications	21	20	95	*
Diversified services	60	57	95	91
Trade	32	30	94	86
Commercial banking	66	60	91	82
Utilities	66	57	86	48
Insurance	67	57	85	68

* Data not available.

Table 5: Prevalence of Bonus Awards

Industry Category		1990	1989*
	Total Plans	Percent that Paid Bonus	Percent that Paid Bonus
Communications	20	100%	88%
Energy	37	97	86
Insurance	57	97	93
Manufacturing	295	94	92
Diversified services	57	91	91
Utilities	57	91	93
Trade	30	83	100
Commercial banking	60	77	86

* From *Top Executive Compensation: 1990 Edition*

Table 6: Median CEO Bonus Awards for 1990

Industry Category	Number of CEOS	Percent of Salary
Energy	25	64%
Diversified services	47	58
Manufacturing	164	55
Trade	23	55
Insurance	54	40
Commercial banking	42	38
Communications	10	35
Utilities	44	32

Table 7: Prevalence of Restricted Stock Plans

Industry Category	May, 1991 Total Companies	With Restricted Stock Number	With Restricted Stock Percent	May, 1986 Percent with Restricted Stock
Energy	37	20	54%	*
Manufacturing	300	138	46	28%
Diversified service	60	25	42	26
Commercial banking	66	27	41	19
Communications	21	8	38	*
Trade	32	10	31	14
Insurance: stock	28	8	29	15
Utilities	66	15	23	7

Data not available.

Table 8: Median Restricted Stock Awards for 1990 to the Five Highest-Paid Executives as a Group

Industry Category*	Number of Companies	Number of Executives	Median (Percent of Salary)
Commercial banking	12	50	81%
Diversified service	7	34	81
Energy	9	39	54
Insurance: stock	5	19	49
Manufacturing	44	181	34
Communications	5	23	27
Trade	3	11	26
Utilities	7	35	23

Table 9: Prevalence of Long-Term Performance Plans

Industry Category	May, 1991 Total Companies	With Long-term Performance Plans Number	With Long-term Performance Plans Percent	May, 1986 Percent with Long-term Performance Plans
Communications	21	10	48%	*
Manfacturing	300	123	41	38%
Energy	37	14	38	*
Trade	32	11	34	19
Insurance	67	21	31	19
Utilities	66	18	27	19
Diversified service	60	12	20	52
Commercial banking	66	12	18	18

* Data not available.

Table 10: Types of Long-Term Performance Plans

Industry Category	Total Plans	Both Unit and Share Plans Number	Both Unit and Share Plans Percent	Only Unit Plan Number	Only Unit Plan Percent	Only Share Plan Number	Only Share Plan Percent
Manufacturing	123	9	7%	73	59%	41	33%
Insurance	21	—	—	16	76	5	24
Utilities	18	2	11	7	39	9	50
Energy	14	—	—	9	64	5	36
Commercial banking	12	1	8	6	50	5	42
Diversified service	12	1	8	6	50	5	42
Trade	11	1	9	7	64	3	27
Communications	10	—	—	8	80	2	20

Table 11: Median Long-Term Performance Awards for 1990 to the Five Highest-Paid Executives as a Group

Industry Category*	Number of Companies	Number of Executives	Median (Percent of Salary)
Energy	5	19	142%
Commercial banking	6	23	80
Manufacturing	44	197	63
Diversified service	9	38	56
Insurance	8	39	44
Trade	7	34	30
Utilities	11	53	25

* Insufficient data for Communications.

Table 12: Median Long-Term Performance Payments for 1990 to the Five Highest-Paid Executives as a Group

Industry Category*	Number of Companies	Number of Executives	Median (Percent of Salary)
Manufacturing	37	169	51%
Diversified service . . .	11	45	48
Commercial banking . .	4	15	35
Energy	7	31	35
Utilities	12	55	34
Insurance	15	69	30
Trade	9	43	23

* Insufficient data for Communications.

Table 13: Prevalence of Stock Option Plans

		May, 1991		May, 1986
	Total	With Stock Option Plan		Percent with Stock
Industry Category	Companies	Number	Percent	Option Plan
Energy	37	35	95%	*
Manufacturing	300	249	83	82%
Communications . . .	21	17	81	*
Trade	32	25	78	73
Commercial banking .	66	50	76	61
Insurance: stock . . .	28	21	75	45
Diversified services . .	60	41	68	100
Utilities	66	34	52	24

*Data not available.

Table 14: Types of Options

		Number and Percent of Plans by Type					
		Both ISO and Nonqualified		Only ISO		Only Nonqualified	
Industry Category	Total Responses	Number	Percent	Number	Percent	Number	Percent
Manufacturing . . .	248	204	82%	6	2%	38	15%
Commercial banking	49	33	67	8	16	8	16
Diversified services	41	29	71	1	2	11	27
Energy	35	24	69	2	6	9	26
Utilities	33	20	61	1	3	12	36
Trade	24	14	58	2	8	8	33
Insurance: stock .	17	6	35	2	12	9	53
Communications .	16	11	69	—	—	5	31

Table 15: 1990 Stock Option Grants

Industry Category	Companies with Stock Option Plan	Granted Options in 1990	
		Number	Percent
Trade	25	20	80%
Commercial banking	50	38	76
Insurance: stock	21	14	67
Energy	35	21	60
Diversified services	41	24	59
Manufacturing	249	141	57
Utilities	34	18	53
Communications	17	6	35

Table 16: 1990 Stock Option Grants by Type

		Type of Option Granted					
	Total	Both ISO and Nonqualifed		ISO Only		Nonqualified Only	
Industry Category	Responses	Number	Percent	Number	Percent	Number	Percent
Manufacturing	134	37	28%	4	3%	93	69%
Commercial banking	35	9	26	4	11	22	63
Diversified service	22	6	27	3	14	13	59
Energy	21	5	24	1	5	15	71
Trade	19	5	26	1	5	13	68
Utilities	18	—	—	—	—	18	100
Insurance: stock	14	3	21	2	14	9	64
Communications	5	—	—	—	—	5	100

Table 17: Incentive Stock Options With Stock Swap—Stock Appreciation Rights

Industry Category	ISO Plans	With Stock Swap		With SAR	
		Number	Percent	Number	Percent
Manufacturing . . .	210	92	44%	45	21%
Commercial banking	41	26	63	12	29
Diversified services	30	22	73	12	40
Energy	26	10	39	11	42
Utilities	21	15	71	7	33
Trade	16	14	88	3	19
Communications .	11	4	36	1	9
Insurance: stock . .	8	4	50	5	63

Table 18: Nonqualified Options With Stock Swap—Stock Appreciation Rights

Industry Category	Nonqualified Options	With Stock Swap		With SAR	
		Number	Percent	Number	Percent
Manufacturing . . .	242	106	44%	51	21%
Commercial banking	41	26	63	11	27
Diversified service .	40	29	73	14	35
Energy	33	16	49	18	55
Utilities	32	22	69	14	44
Trade	22	14	64	6	27
Communications .	16	5	31	1	6
Insurance: stock . .	15	7	47	6	40

Table 19: Size of 1990 Stock Option Grants to the Five Highest-Paid Executives as a Group

Industry Category	Number of Companies	Number of Executives	Size of Grant (Percent of Salary)		
			Median	Middle 50% Range	
				Low	High
Diversified service . . .	20	82	184%	92%	241%
Communications . . .	6	30	165	106	233
Utilities	18	88	160	93	255
Energy	20	96	158	103	232
Manufacturing	129	607	130	78	228
Insurance: stock	12	58	121	79	224
Commercial banking .	33	160	107	62	197
Trade	18	82	99	53	181

Table 20: Gains at Exercise in 1990 of the Five Highest-Paid Executives as a Group

Industry Category*	Number of Companies	Number of Executives	Dollars			Percent of Salary		
			Median	Middle 50% Range		Median	Middle 50% Range	
				Low	High		Low	High
Commerical Banking	13	30	$286,000	$63,000	$757,000	81%	23%	178%
Manufacturing	48	139	273,000	84,000	610,000	68	27	164
Trade	10	28	255,000	83,000	568,000	58	28	147
Energy	11	30	190,000	62,000	736,000	63	25	157
Utilities	7	21	155,000	22,000	336,000	72	6	102
Diversified service	9	18	147,000	72,000	567,000	53	30	107

* Insufficient data for Communications and Insurance.

Compensation by Industry Category

The balance of the report contains the information listed below for each of the eight major industry categories and for 13 manufacturing sub-categories:

- Distribution of companies according to size;

- Median, low and high of middle 50 percent range for total current compensation and salary;

- Regression formulas for total current compensation and salary;

- Charts showing regression lines measuring the relationship between total current compensation and company size; and

- Total current compensation and salary of the second through fifth highest-paid executives as a percentage of CEO pay.

Each major industry section also contains an analysis relating bonus awards to company size and a table showing the size of bonus awards for each of the five executives, with the exception of communications, where data were insufficient for analysis. Life insurance and property and casualty insurance are analyzed in separate sections.

Executive Pay and Company Size

The regression line charts and the regression formulas are based on the generally accepted belief that a positive correlation exists between company size and executive pay. The CEO of a large company is paid more than the CEO of a small company because the large company CEO has a more difficult and demanding job.

The regression lines on the charts measure the general relationship between total current compensation and company size. The lines can be used for determining the average compensation of executives according to company size. For greater precision, the regression formulas can be used. (See the Appendix on page 67 for an explanation of how to use the formulas.)

Manufacturing

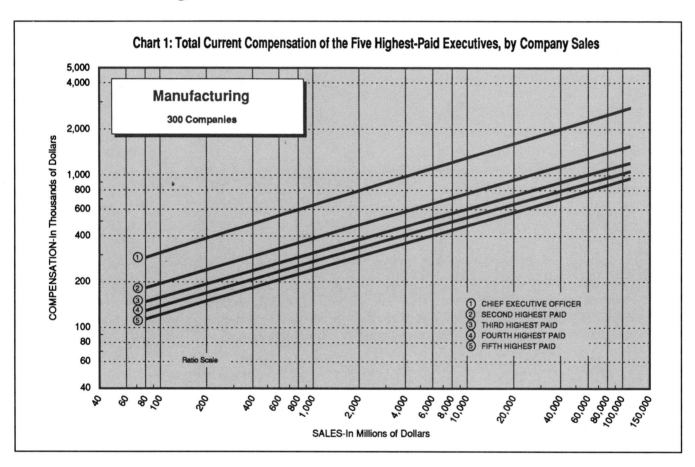

Chart 1: Total Current Compensation of the Five Highest-Paid Executives, by Company Sales

Manufacturing

300 Companies

COMPENSATION-In Thousands of Dollars

Ratio Scale

① CHIEF EXECUTIVE OFFICER
② SECOND HIGHEST PAID
③ THIRD HIGHEST PAID
④ FOURTH HIGHEST PAID
⑤ FIFTH HIGHEST PAID

SALES-In Millions of Dollars

Table 21: 1990 Sales Volume

1990 Sales	Companies	
	Number	Percent
$5 billion and over	72	24%
2-4,999 billion	60	20
1-1,999 billion	54	18
500-999 million	58	19
300-499 million	26	9
200-299 million	18	6
199 million and under	12	4
TOTAL	300	100%

Median	Middle 50% Range	
	Low	High
$1.6 billion	$621 million	$4.7 billion

Table 22: 1990 Total Current Compensation

Compensation Rank	Median	Middle 50% Range	
		Low	High
CEO	$730,000	$462,000	$1,127,000
Second highest	449,000	305,000	655,000
Third highest	361,000	239,000	507,000
Fourth highest	319,000	212,000	450,000
Fifth highest	276,000	189,000	400,000

Table 23: 1990 Total Current Compensation Regression Formula

Compensation Rank	Formula	r^2
CEO	$\log Y = 1.8680 + 0.3110 \log X$	46%
Second highest	$\log Y = 1.7000 + 0.2950 \log X$	52
Third highest	$\log Y = 1.6190 + 0.2890 \log X$	55
Fourth highest	$\log Y = 1.5590 + 0.2900 \log X$	58
Fifth highest	$\log Y = 1.5010 + 0.2930 \log X$	59

Table 24: Total Current Compensation as a Percentage of CEO's Total Current Compensation

Compensation Rank	Median	Middle 50% Range	
		Low	High
Second highest	64%	52%	75%
Third highest	50	40	58
Fourth highest	43	37	51
Fifth highest	38	33	46

Table 25: 1990 Salary

Compensation Rank	Median	Middle 50% Range	
		Low	High
CEO	$482,000	$325,000	$650,000
Second highest	286,000	204,000	395,000
Third highest	240,000	175,000	317,000
Fourth highest	218,000	157,000	291,000
Fifth highest	192,000	144,000	265,000

Table 26: 1990 Salary Regression Formula

Compensation Rank	Formula	r^2
CEO	$\log Y = 1.8590 + 0.2520 \log X$	63%
Second highest	$\log Y = 1.6660 + 0.2480 \log X$	62
Third highest	$\log Y = 1.6100 + 0.2390 \log X$	66
Fourth highest	$\log Y = 1.5540 + 0.2440 \log X$	71
Fifth highest	$\log Y = 1.5330 + 0.2370 \log X$	71

Table 27: Salary as a Percentage of CEO's Salary

Compensation Rank	Median	Middle 50% Range	
		Low	High
Second highest	61%	53%	74%
Third highest	52	44	60
Fourth highest	46	40	53
Fifth highest	42	37	49

Table 28: 1990 Bonus Awards (as Percent of Salary) by Company Size

Executive	Sales Volume		
	Middle 50% Range		
	Low $621 Million	Median $1.6 Billion	High $4.7 Billion
CEO			
1990 Bonus	49%	57%	68%
Salary	$366,000	$468,000	$618,000
Second Highest			
1990 Bonus	45%	53%	64%
Salary	$228,000	$289,000	$377,000
Third Highest			
1990 Bonus	39%	48%	59%
Salary	$189,000	$238,000	$309,000
Fourth Highest			
1990 Bonus	37%	44%	54%
Salary	$170,000	$216,000	$283,000
Fifth Highest			
1990 Bonus	33%	42%	54%
Salary	$155,000	$196,000	$255,000

Table 29: 1990 Bonus Awards

1990 Bonus Awards (Percent of Salary)	CEOS		Second Highest Paid		Third Highest Paid		Fourth Highest Paid		Fifth Highest Paid	
	Number	Percent	Number	Percent	Number	Percent	Number	Percent	Number	Percent
100% or more	32	20%	19	12%	16	10%	12	7%	10	6%
90-99	8	5	9	6	3	2	3	2	6	4
80-89	9	6	6	4	6	4	8	5	6	4
70-79	15	9	12	7	13	8	7	4	5	3
60-69	12	7	19	12	13	8	14	9	13	8
50-59	26	16	20	12	27	16	26	16	27	16
40-49	19	12	31	19	30	18	29	18	26	16
30-39	14	9	24	15	20	12	23	14	28	17
20-29	14	9	9	6	19	11	22	13	18	11
10-19	12	7	12	7	15	9	15	9	16	10
Less than 10%	3	2	3	2	5	3	6	4	11	7
Total	164	100%	164	100%	167	100%	165	100%	166	100%
Median Bonus	55%		50%		48%		45%		44%	
Middle 50% Range	37—87%		37—72%		32—65%		29—60%		27—59%	

Individual Manufacturing Industries

Aerospace

Chart 2: Total Current Compensation of the Five Highest-Paid Executives, by Company Sales

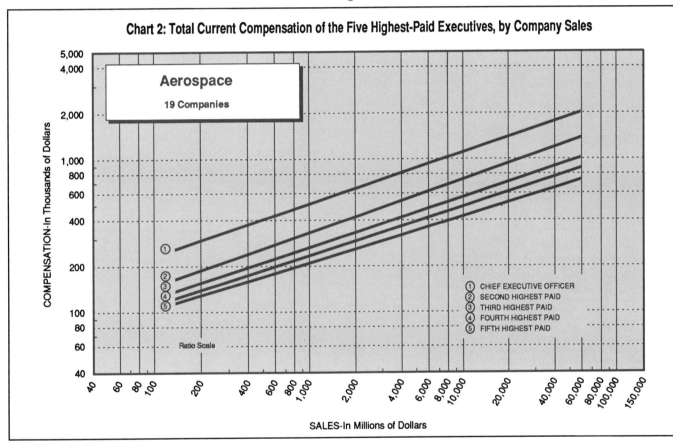

Table 30: 1990 Sales Volume

	Companies	
1990 Sales	Number	Percent
$5 billion and over	9	47%
2-4,999 billion	2	11
1-1,999 billion	3	16
500-999 million	—	—
300-499 million	2	11
200-299 million	2	11
199 million and under	1	5
Total	19	100%

	Middle 50% Range	
Median	Low	High
$4.0 billion	$340 million	$10.2 billion

Table 31: 1990 Total Current Compensation

		Middle 50% Range	
Compensation Rank	Median	Low	High
CEO	$821,000	$323,000	$1,095,000
Second highest	547,000	248,000	785,000
Third highest	428,000	212,000	650,000
Fourth highest	385,000	158,000	577,000
Fifth highest	347,000	154,000	428,000

Table 32: 1990 Total Current Compensation Regression Formula

Compensation Rank	Formula	r^2
CEO	log Y = 1.6940 + 0.3370 log X	72%
Second highest	log Y = 1.4710 + 0.3490 log X	76
Third highest	log Y = 1.4340 + 0.3290 log X	76
Fourth highest	log Y = 1.4030 + 0.3220 log X	78
Fifth highest	log Y = 1.4030 + 0.3060 log X	74

Table 33: Total Current Compensation as a Percentage of CEO's Total Current Compensation

Compensation Rank	Median	Middle 50% Range	
		Low	High
Second highest	67%	57%	75%
Third highest	52	42	65
Fourth highest	47	38	52
Fifth highest	38	34	49

Table 34: 1990 Salary

Compensation Rank	Median	Middle 50% Range	
		Low	High
CEO	$595,000	$260,000	$855,000
Second highest	375,000	193,000	502,000
Third highest	290,000	174,000	453,000
Fourth highest	281,000	177,000	403,000
Fifth highest	275,000	155,000	322,000

Table 35: 1990 Salary Regression Formula

Compensation Rank	Formula	r^2
CEO	log Y = 1.8950 + 0.2380 log X	56%
Second highest	log Y = 1.5870 + 0.2730 log X	67
Third highest	log Y = 1.5900 + 0.2450 log X	63
Fourth highest	log Y = 1.5560 + 0.2500 log X	73
Fifth highest	log Y = 1.6350 + 0.2070 log X	61

Table 36: Salary as a Percentage of CEO's Salary

Compensation Rank	Median	Middle 50% Range	
		Low	High
Second highest	62%	56%	69%
Third highest	53	45	59
Fourth highest	46	40	51
Fifth highest	42	35	50

Computer Hardware and Office Equipment

Chart 3: Total Current Compensation of the Five Highest-Paid Executives, by Company Sales

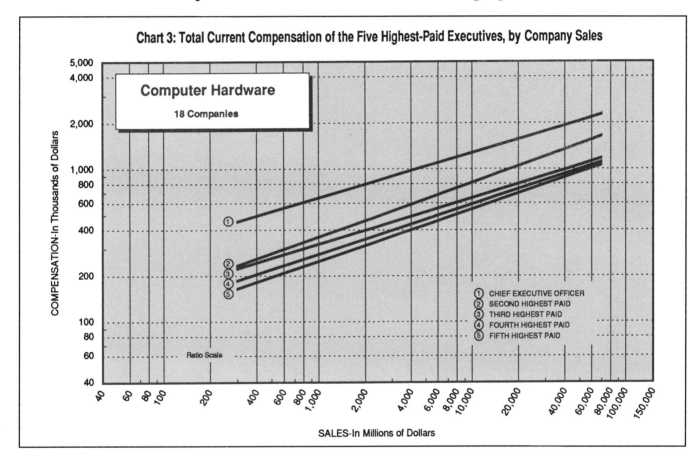

Table 37: 1990 Sales Volume

1990 Sales	Companies	
	Number	Percent
$5 billion and over	7	39%
2-4,999 billion	4	22
1-1,999 billion	3	17
500-999 million	2	11
300-499 million	1	6
299 million and under	1	6
Total	18	100%

Median	Middle 50% Range	
	Low	High
$2.5 billion	$1.1 billion	$10.1 billion

Table 38: 1990 Total Current Compensation

Compensation Rank	Median	Middle 50% Range	
		Low	High
CEO	$925,000	$584,000	$1,295,000
Second highest	537,000	354,000	975,000
Third highest	462,000	326,000	690,000
Fourth highest	388,000	304,000	620,000
Fifth highest	356,000	241,000	603,000

Table 39: 1990 Total Current Compensation Regression Formula

Compensation Rank	Formula	r^2
CEO	log Y = 1.9310 + 0.2940 log X	45%
Second highest	log Y = 1.4520 + 0.3640 log X	69
Third highest	log Y = 1.6020 + 0.3030 log X	58
Fourth highest	log Y = 1.4640 + 0.3260 log X	64
Fifth highest	log Y = 1.3700 + 0.3420 log X	68

Table 40: Total Current Compensation as a Percentage of CEO's Total Current Compensation

Compensation Rank	Median	Middle 50% Range	
		Low	High
Second highest	60%	52%	70%
Third highest	50	39	66
Fourth highest	43	35	60
Fifth highest	39	31	59

Table 41: 1990 Salary

Compensation Rank	Median	Middle 50% Range	
		Low	High
CEO	$585,000	$450,000	$700,000
Second highest	329,000	228,000	496,000
Third highest	250,000	220,000	350,000
Fourth highest	255,000	185,000	340,000
Fifth highest	184,000	157,000	350,000

Table 42: 1990 Salary Regression Formula

Compensation Rank	Formula	r^2
CEO	log Y = 2.1120 + 0.1810 log X	51%
Second highest	log Y = 1.6920 + 0.2330 log X	74
Third highest	log Y = 1.9530 + 0.1390 log X	66
Fourth highest	log Y = 1.7650 + 0.1800 log X	74
Fifth highest	log Y = 1.6370 + 0.2060 log X	67

Table 43: Salary as a Percentage of CEO's Salary

Compensation Rank	Median	Middle 50% Range	
		Low	High
Second highest	57%	47%	60%
Third highest	49	40	54
Fourth highest	41	39	53
Fifth highest	41	28	64

Consumer Chemicals

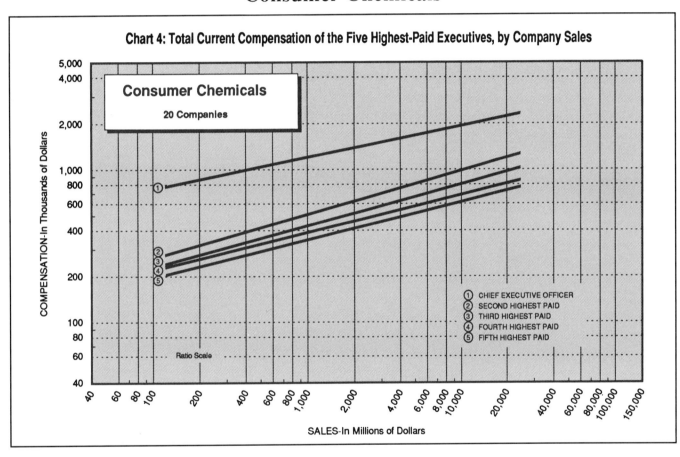

Chart 4: Total Current Compensation of the Five Highest-Paid Executives, by Company Sales

Consumer Chemicals

20 Companies

COMPENSATION-In Thousands of Dollars

Ratio Scale

① CHIEF EXECUTIVE OFFICER
② SECOND HIGHEST PAID
③ THIRD HIGHEST PAID
④ FOURTH HIGHEST PAID
⑤ FIFTH HIGHEST PAID

SALES-In Millions of Dollars

Table 44: 1990 Sales Volume

1990 Sales	Companies	
	Number	Percent
$5 billion and over	8	40%
2-4,999 billion	5	25
1-1,999 billion	3	15
500-999 million	1	5
300-499 million	2	10
200-299 million	—	—
199 million and under	1	5
Total	20	100%

Median	Middle 50% Range	
	Low	High
$3.5 billion	$1.2 billion	$6.2 billion

Table 45: 1990 Total Current Compensation

Compensation Rank	Median	Middle 50% Range	
		Low	High
CEO	$1,506,000	$940,000	$2,120,000
Second highest	698,000	468,000	945,000
Third highest	556,000	422,000	698,000
Fourth highest	517,000	386,000	643,000
Fifth highest	414,000	341,000	630,000

Table 46: 1990 Total Current Compensation Regression Formula

Compensation Rank	Formula	r^2
CEO	log Y = 2.4610 + 0.2060 log X	19%
Second highest	log Y = 1.8510 + 0.2850 log X	64
Third highest	log Y = 1.7880 + 0.2780 log X	81
Fourth highest	log Y = 1.8710 + 0.2410 log X	70
Fifth highest	log Y = 1.7860 + 0.2500 log X	71

Table 47: Total Current Compensation as a Percentage of CEO's Total Current Compensation

Compensation Rank	Median	Middle 50% Range	
		Low	High
Second highest	53%	30%	74%
Third highest	43	27	51
Fourth highest	41	25	49
Fifth highest	38	26	42

Table 48: 1990 Salary

Compensation Rank	Median	Middle 50% Range	
		Low	High
CEO	$800,000	$440,000	$1,008,000
Second highest	504,000	286,000	553,000
Third highest	385,000	293,000	504,000
Fourth highest	385,000	275,000	442,000
Fifth highest	325,000	221,000	442,000

Table 49: 1990 Salary Regression Formula

Compensation Rank	Formula	r^2
CEO	log Y = 1.7270+ 0.3190 log X	79%
Second highest	log Y = 1.8110 + 0.2460 log X	54
Third highest	log Y = 1.6900 + 0.2530 log X	77
Fourth highest	log Y = 1.7180 + 0.2350 log X	73
Fifth highest	log Y = 1.5380 + 0.2740 log X	75

Table 50: Salary as a Percentage of CEO's Salary

Compensation Rank	Median	Middle 50% Range	
		Low	High
Second highest	69%	59%	86%
Third highest	56	46	66
Fourth highest	51	44	57
Fifth highest	47	41	50

Electrical and Electronic Machinery

Chart 5: Total Current Compensation of the Five Highest-Paid Executives, by Company Sales

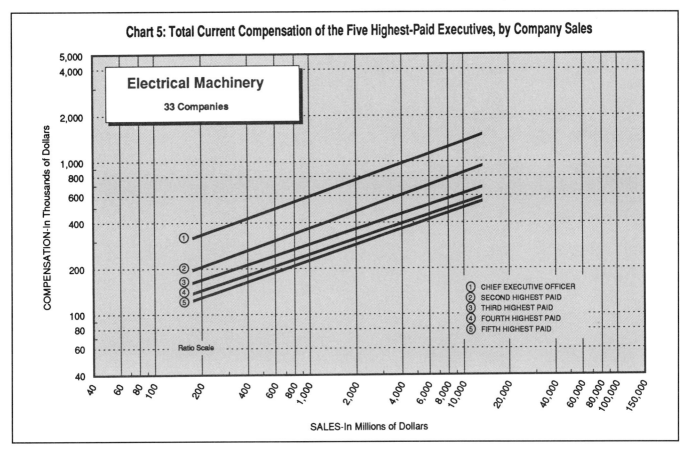

Table 51: 1990 Sales Volume

1990 Sales	Companies	
	Number	Percent
$5 billion and over	7	21%
2-4,999 billion	5	15
1-1,999 billion	5	15
500-999 million	10	30
300-499 million	2	6
200-299 million	2	6
199 million and under	2	6
Total	33	100%

Median	Middle 50% Range	
	Low	High
$1.2 billion	$602 million	$3.1 billion

Table 52: 1990 Total Current Compensation

Compensation Rank	Median	Middle 50% Range	
		Low	High
CEO	$642,000	$429,000	$1,021,000
Second highest	347,000	280,000	712,000
Third highest	295,000	219,000	462,000
Fourth highest	259,000	170,000	435,000
Fifth highest	211,000	164,000	413,000

Table 53: 1990 Total Current Compensation Regression Formula

Compensation Rank	Formula	r^2
CEO	log Y = 1.6790 + 0.3660 log X	61%
Second highest	log Y = 1.4640 + 0.3680 log X	50
Third highest	log Y = 1.4470 + 0.3380 log X	49
Fourth highest	log Y = 1.3660 + 0.3430 log X	57
Fifth highest	log Y = 1.3010 + 0.3520 log X	59

Table 54: Total Current Compensation as a Percentage of CEO's Total Current Compensation

Compensation Rank	Median	Middle 50% Range	
		Low	High
Second highest	62%	51%	80%
Third highest	48	40	57
Fourth highest	40	35	49
Fifth highest	37	32	45

Table 55: 1990 Salary

Compensation Rank	Median	Middle 50% Range	
		Low	High
CEO	$485,000	$316,000	$650,000
Second highest	265,000	182,000	347,000
Third highest	230,000	161,000	268,000
Fourth highest	195,000	147,000	266,000
Fifth highest	160,000	134,000	266,000

Table 56: 1990 Salary Regression Formula

Compensation Rank	Formula	r^2
CEO	log Y = 1.8850 + 0.2430 log X	67%
Second highest	log Y = 1.7080 + 0.2210 log X	55
Third highest	log Y = 1.6360 + 0.2230 log X	65
Fourth highest	log Y = 1.5220 + 0.2490 log X	62
Fifth highest	log Y = 1.5420 + 0.2250 log X	74

Table 57: Salary as a Percentage of CEO's Salary

Compensation Rank	Median	Middle 50% Range	
		Low	High
Second highest	56%	48%	74%
Third highest	47	41	58
Fourth highest	44	39	52
Fifth highest	41	32	48

Fabricated Metal Products

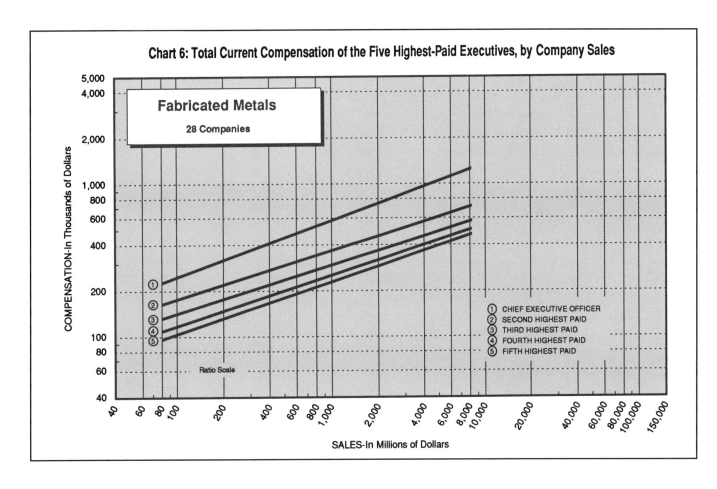

Chart 6: Total Current Compensation of the Five Highest-Paid Executives, by Company Sales

Fabricated Metals

28 Companies

COMPENSATION-In Thousands of Dollars

Ratio Scale

① CHIEF EXECUTIVE OFFICER
② SECOND HIGHEST PAID
③ THIRD HIGHEST PAID
④ FOURTH HIGHEST PAID
⑤ FIFTH HIGHEST PAID

SALES-In Millions of Dollars

Table 58: 1990 Sales Volume

1990 Sales	Companies	
	Number	Percent
$5 billion and over	3	11%
2-4,999 billion	5	18
1-1,999 billion	5	18
500-999 million	5	18
300-499 million	5	18
200-299 million	2	7
199 million and under	3	11
Total	28	100%

Median	Middle 50% Range	
	Low	High
$589 million	$356 million	$2.5 billion

Table 59: 1990 Total Current Compensation

Compensation Rank	Median	Middle 50% Range	
		Low	High
CEO	$630,000	$338,000	$885,000
Second highest	430,000	229,000	552,000
Third highest	284,000	189,000	436,000
Fourth highest	251,000	161,000	343,000
Fifth highest	226,000	145,000	331,000

Table 60: 1990 Total Current Compensation Regression Formula

Compensation Rank	Formula	r^2
CEO	log Y = 1.6360 + 0.3790 log X	76%
Second highest	log Y = 1.5990 + 0.3250 log X	52
Third highest	log Y = 1.4980 + 0.3270 log X	61
Fourth highest	log Y = 1.3920 + 0.3400 log X	72
Fifth highest	log Y = 1.3110 + 0.3520 log X	75

Table 61: Total Current Compensation as a Percentage of CEO's Total Current Compensation

Compensation Rank	Median	Middle 50% Range	
		Low	High
Second highest	66%	54%	73%
Third highest	53	43	59
Fourth highest	47	38	51
Fifth highest	39	34	48

Table 62: 1990 Salary

Compensation Rank	Median	Middle 50% Range	
		Low	High
CEO	$371,000	$225,000	$551,000
Second highest	257,000	165,000	330,000
Third highest	200,000	146,000	285,000
Fourth highest	177,000	128,000	232,000
Fifth highest	150,000	121,000	210,000

Table 63: 1990 Salary Regression Formula

Compensation Rank	Formula	r^2
CEO	log Y = 1.7770 + 0.2690 log X	70%
Second highest	log Y = 1.7450 + 0.3250 log X	48
Third highest	log Y = 1.6520 + 0.2240 log X	58
Fourth highest	log Y = 1.5490 + 0.2370 log X	71
Fifth highest	log Y = 1.4840 + 0.2450 log X	80

Table 64: Salary as a Percentage of CEO's Salary

Compensation Rank	Median	Middle 50% Range	
		Low	High
Second highest	66%	60%	76%
Third highest	57	50	60
Fourth highest	49	44	54
Fifth highest	42	39	49

Food and Kindred Products

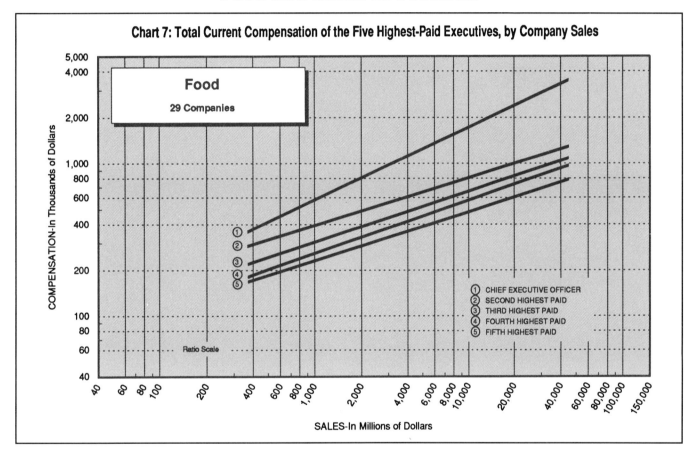

Chart 7: Total Current Compensation of the Five Highest-Paid Executives, by Company Sales

Food
29 Companies

① CHIEF EXECUTIVE OFFICER
② SECOND HIGHEST PAID
③ THIRD HIGHEST PAID
④ FOURTH HIGHEST PAID
⑤ FIFTH HIGHEST PAID

COMPENSATION-In Thousands of Dollars

Ratio Scale

SALES-In Millions of Dollars

Table 65: 1990 Sales Volume

1990 Sales	Companies	
	Number	Percent
$5 billion and over	12	41%
2-4,999 billion	4	14
1-1,999 billion	6	21
500-999 million	6	21
300-499 million	1	3
Total	29	100%

Median	Middle 50% Range	
	Low	High
$2.7 billion	$1.1 billion	$7.6 billion

Table 66: 1990 Total Current Compensation

Compensation Rank	Median	Middle 50% Range	
		Low	High
CEO	$960,000	$530,000	$1,617,000
Second highest	620,000	388,000	869,000
Third highest	440,000	293,000	664,000
Fourth highest	403,000	283,000	545,000
Fifth highest	334,000	276,000	514,000

Table 67: 1990 Total Current Compensation Regression Formula

Compensation Rank	Formula	r^2
CEO	log Y = 1.3310 + 0.4760 log X	65%
Second highest	log Y = 1.6550 + 0.3130 log X	49
Third highest	log Y = 1.4920 + 0.3310 log X	51
Fourth highest	log Y = 1.3540 + 0.3510 log X	63
Fifth highest	log Y = 1.4020 + 0.3210 log X	58

Table 68: Total Current Compensation as a Percentage of CEO's Total Current Compensation

Compensation Rank	Median	Middle 50% Range	
		Low	High
Second highest	68%	45%	79%
Third highest	50	34	61
Fourth highest	42	31	51
Fifth highest	35	25	45

Table 69: 1990 Salary

Compensation Rank	Median	Middle 50% Range	
		Low	High
CEO	$485,000	$328,000	$783,000
Second highest	371,000	271,000	510,000
Third highest	320,000	214,000	446,000
Fourth highest	275,000	214,000	372,000
Fifth highest	220,000	183,000	290,000

Table 70: 1990 Salary Regression Formula

Compensation Rank	Formula	r^2
CEO	log Y = 1.2890 + 0.4040 log X	76%
Second highest	log Y = 1.2010 + 0.3850 log X	62
Third highest	log Y = 1.3680 + 0.3170 log X	61
Fourth highest	log Y = 1.4930 + 0.2690 log X	53
Fifth highest	log Y = 1.4440 + 0.2620 log X	56

Table 71: Salary as a Percentage of CEO's Salary

Compensation Rank	Median	Middle 50% Range	
		Low	High
Second highest	72%	54%	85%
Third highest	54	47	71
Fourth highest	51	42	67
Fifth highest	45	36	61

Industrial Chemicals

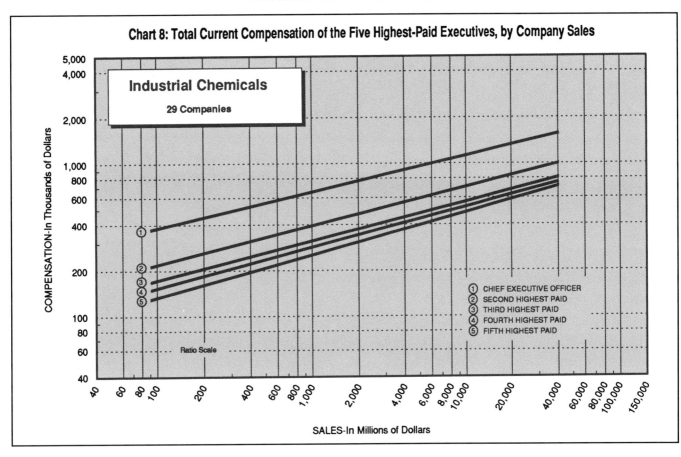

Chart 8: Total Current Compensation of the Five Highest-Paid Executives, by Company Sales

Industrial Chemicals

29 Companies

COMPENSATION-In Thousands of Dollars

Ratio Scale

① CHIEF EXECUTIVE OFFICER
② SECOND HIGHEST PAID
③ THIRD HIGHEST PAID
④ FOURTH HIGHEST PAID
⑤ FIFTH HIGHEST PAID

SALES-In Millions of Dollars

Table 72: 1990 Sales Volume

1990 Sales	Companies	
	Number	Percent
$5 billion and over	6	21%
2-4,999 billion	5	17
1-1,999 billion	8	28
500-999 million	4	14
300-499 million	2	7
200-299 million	3	10
199 million and under	1	3
Total	29	100%

Median	Middle 50% Range	
	Low	High
$1.6 billion	$719 million	$3.2 billion

Table 73: 1990 Total Current Compensation

Compensation Rank	Median	Middle 50% Range	
		Low	High
CEO	$707,000	$484,000	$1,169,000
Second highest	416,000	300,000	651,000
Third highest	340,000	241,000	469,000
Fourth highest	318,000	221,000	429,000
Fifth highest	287,000	191,000	391,000

Table 74: 1990 Total Current Compensation Regression Formula

Compensation Rank	Formula	r^2
CEO	log Y = 2.1070 + 0.2360 log X	48%
Second highest	log Y = 1.8370 + 0.2520 log X	48
Third highest	log Y = 1.7260 + 0.2560 log X	53
Fourth highest	log Y = 1.6570 + 0.2640 log X	60
Fifth highest	log Y = 1.5700 + 0.2790 log X	60

Table 75: Total Current Compensation as a Percentage of CEO's Total Current Compensation

Compensation Rank	Median	Middle 50% Range	
		Low	High
Second highest	64%	54%	71%
Third highest	52	41	56
Fourth highest	46	38	51
Fifth highest	41	34	48

Table 76: 1990 Salary

Compensation Rank	Median	Middle 50% Range	
		Low	High
CEO	$443,000	$356,000	$656,000
Second highest	281,000	205,000	438,000
Third highest	227,000	184,000	293,000
Fourth highest	215,000	170,000	264,000
Fifth highest	196,000	147,000	261,000

Table 77: 1990 Salary Regression Formula

Compensation Rank	Formula	r^2
CEO	log Y = 2.0810 + 0.1820 log X	56%
Second highest	log Y = 1.7910 + 0.2110 log X	64
Third highest	log Y = 1.5970 + 0.2420 log X	78
Fourth highest	log Y = 1.5590 + 0.2410 log X	83
Fifth highest	log Y = 1.5930 + 0.2250 log X	77

Table 78: Salary as a Percentage of CEO's Salary

Compensation Rank	Median	Middle 50% Range	
		Low	High
Second highest	63%	54%	73%
Third highest	53	45	60
Fourth highest	47	39	56
Fifth highest	47	40	52

Machinery (except Electrical)

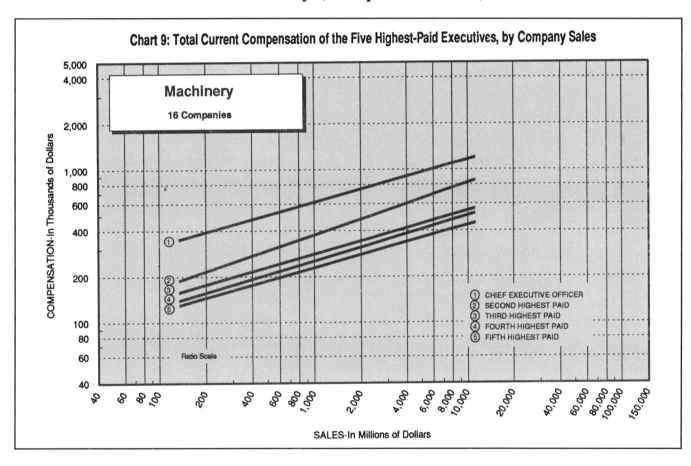

Chart 9: Total Current Compensation of the Five Highest-Paid Executives, by Company Sales

Machinery

16 Companies

COMPENSATION-In Thousands of Dollars

Ratio Scale

① CHIEF EXECUTIVE OFFICER
② SECOND HIGHEST PAID
③ THIRD HIGHEST PAID
④ FOURTH HIGHEST PAID
⑤ FIFTH HIGHEST PAID

SALES-In Millions of Dollars

Table 79: 1990 Sales Volume

	Companies	
1990 Sales	*Number*	*Percent*
$5 billion and over	3	19%
2-4,999 billion	3	19
1-1,999 billion	3	19
500-999 million	3	19
300-499 million	2	13
200-299 million	1	6
199 million and under	1	6
Total	16	100%

	Middle 50% Range	
Median	Low	High
$1 billion	$453 million	$2.5 billion

Table 80: 1990 Total Current Compensation

		Middle 50% Range	
Compensation Rank	*Median*	*Low*	*High*
CEO	$531,000	$440,000	$1,184,000
Second highest	420,000	268,000	610,000
Third highest	268,000	222,000	417,000
Fourth highest	254,000	210,000	370,000
Fifth highest	246,000	179,000	350,000

Table 81: 1990 Total Current Compensation Regression Formula

Compensation Rank	Formula	r^2
CEO	log Y = 1.9580 + 0.2770 log X	35%
Second highest	log Y = 1.5550 + 0.3390 log X	53
Third highest	log Y = 1.5950 + 0.2840 log X	54
Fourth highest	log Y = 1.5160 + 0.2960 log X	58
Fifth highest	log Y = 1.5250 + 0.2780 log X	59

Table 82: Total Current Compensation as a Percentage of CEO's Total Current Compensation

Compensation Rank	Median	Middle 50% Range	
		Low	High
Second highest	63%	47%	82%
Third highest	50	37	57
Fourth highest	45	31	54
Fifth highest	39	31	48

Table 83: 1990 Salary

Compensation Rank	Median	Middle 50% Range	
		Low	High
CEO	$401,000	$320,000	$550,000
Second highest	226,000	178,000	360,000
Third highest	190,000	159,000	260,000
Fourth highest	175,000	134,000	239,000
Fifth highest	165,000	131,000	230,000

Table 84: 1990 Salary Regression Formula

Compensation Rank	Formula	r^2
CEO	log Y = 1.8990 + 0.2450 log X	54%
Second highest	log Y = 1.6290 + 0.2500 log X	72
Third highest	log Y = 1.6330 + 0.2230 log X	84
Fourth highest	log Y = 1.5310 + 0.2430 log X	87
Fifth highest	log Y = 1.6310 + 0.2030 log X	76

Table 85: Salary as a Percentage of CEO's Salary

Compensation Rank	Median	Middle 50% Range	
		Low	High
Second highest	57%	44%	65%
Third highest	49	35	55
Fourth highest	41	32	51
Fifth highest	41	30	48

Paper

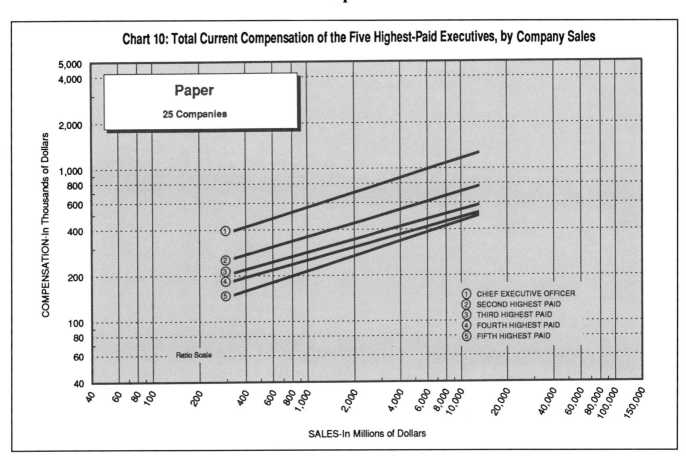

Chart 10: Total Current Compensation of the Five Highest-Paid Executives, by Company Sales

Paper

25 Companies

COMPENSATION-In Thousands of Dollars

① CHIEF EXECUTIVE OFFICER
② SECOND HIGHEST PAID
③ THIRD HIGHEST PAID
④ FOURTH HIGHEST PAID
⑤ FIFTH HIGHEST PAID

Ratio Scale

SALES-In Millions of Dollars

Table 86: 1990 Sales Volume

1990 Sales Volume	Companies	
	Number	Percent
$5 billion and over	8	32%
2-4,999 billion	5	20
1-1,999 billion	4	16
500-999 million	7	28
499 million and under	1	4
Total	25	100%

	Middle 50% Range	
Median	Low	High
$2.4 billion	$841 million	$5.4 billion

Table 87: 1990 Total Current Compensation

Compensation Rank	Median	Middle 50% Range	
		Low	High
CEO	$668,000	$553,000	$1,067,000
Second highest	448,000	334,000	676,000
Third highest	361,000	253,000	528,000
Fourth highest	307,000	244,000	447,000
Fifth highest	256,000	213,000	438,000

Table 88: 1990 Total Current Compensation Regression Formula

Compensation Rank	Formula	r^2
CEO	log Y = 1.7840 + 0.3230 log X	50%
Second highest	log Y = 1.6640 + 0.2980 log X	51
Third highest	log Y = 1.6110 + 0.2820 log X	52
Fourth highest	log Y = 1.5560 + 0.2820 log X	49
Fifth highest	log Y = 1.3500 + 0.3290 log X	58

Table 89: Total Current Compensation as a Percentage of CEO's Total Current Compensation

Compensation Rank	Median	Middle 50% Range	
		Low	High
Second highest	64%	54%	72%
Third highest	50	42	56
Fourth highest	40	39	51
Fifth highest	37	35	44

Table 90: 1990 Salary

Compensation Rank	Median	Middle 50% Range	
		Low	High
CEO	$554,000	$414,000	$800,000
Second highest	330,000	257,000	425,000
Third highest	288,000	204,000	330,000
Fourth highest	241,000	163,000	315,000
Fifth highest	230,000	154,000	300,000

Table 91: 1990 Salary Regression Formula

Compensation Rank	Formula	r^2
CEO	log Y = 1.6140 + 0.3400 log X	68%
Second highest	log Y = 1.4890 + 0.3060 log X	65
Third highest	log Y = 1.5860 + 0.2470 log X	56
Fourth highest	log Y = 1.4970 + 0.2600 log X	70
Fifth highest	log Y = 1.3420 + 0.2960 log X	75

Table 92: Salary as a Percentage of CEO's Salary

Compensation Rank	Median	Middle 50% Range	
		Low	High
Second highest	59%	52%	70%
Third highest	45	43	53
Fourth highest	40	39	45
Fifth highest	38	35	43

Plastic, Rubber and Leather Products

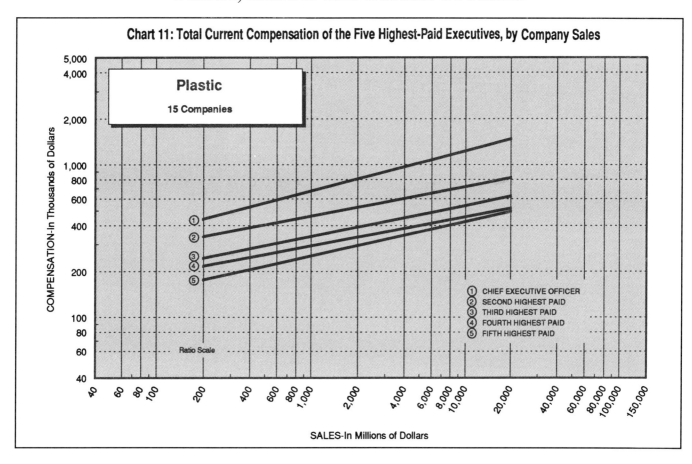

Chart 11: Total Current Compensation of the Five Highest-Paid Executives, by Company Sales

Plastic

15 Companies

COMPENSATION-In Thousands of Dollars

Ratio Scale

1 CHIEF EXECUTIVE OFFICER
2 SECOND HIGHEST PAID
3 THIRD HIGHEST PAID
4 FOURTH HIGHEST PAID
5 FIFTH HIGHEST PAID

SALES-In Millions of Dollars

Table 93: 1990 Sales Volume

1990 Sales	Companies	
	Number	Percent
$5 billion and over	2	13%
2-4,999 billion	1	7
1-1,999 billion	6	40
500-999 million	3	20
300-499 million	2	13
200-299 million	—	—
199 million and under	1	7
Total	15	100%

	Middle 50% Range	
Median	Low	High
$1.3 billion	$586 million	$1.5 billion

Table 94: 1990 Total Current Compensation

Compensation Rank	Median	Middle 50% Range	
		Low	High
CEO	$800,000	$410,000	$1,037,000
Second highest	508,000	325,000	615,000
Third highest	364,000	254,000	496,000
Fourth highest	322,000	230,000	403,000
Fifth highest	303,000	202,000	364,000

Table 95: 1990 Total Current Compensation Regression Formula

Compensation Rank	Formula	r^2
CEO	log Y = 2.0340 + 0.2650 log X	25%
Second highest	log Y = 2.0850 + 0.1930 log X	22
Third highest	log Y = 1.9220 + 0.2030 log X	34
Fourth highest	log Y = 1.8930 + 0.1920 log X	37
Fifth highest	log Y = 1.7260 + 0.2260 log X	45

Table 96: Total Current Compensation as a Percentage of CEO's Total Current Compensation

Compensation Rank	Median	Middle 50% Range	
		Low	High
Second highest	62%	56%	91%
Third highest	51	43	59
Fourth highest	42	37	56
Fifth highest	39	31	46

Table 97: 1990 Salary

Compensation Rank	Median	Middle 50% Range	
		Low	High
CEO	$515,000	$280,000	$703,000
Second highest	309,000	205,000	421,000
Third highest	264,000	160,000	355,000
Fourth highest	224,000	158,000	321,000
Fifth highest	187,000	136,000	271,000

Table 98: 1990 Salary Regression Formula

Compensation Rank	Formula	r^2
CEO	log Y = 1.8370 + 0.2590 log X	58%
Second highest	log Y = 1.6500 + 0.2580 log X	77
Third highest	log Y = 1.5090 + 0.2730 log X	73
Fourth highest	log Y = 1.6770 + 0.2120 log X	68
Fifth highest	log Y = 1.4620 + 0.2550 log X	75

Table 99: Salary as a Percentage of CEO's Salary

Compensation Rank	Median	Middle 50% Range	
		Low	High
Second highest	63%	54%	87%
Third highest	54	44	62
Fourth highest	48	40	57
Fifth highest	42	34	48

Precision Instruments

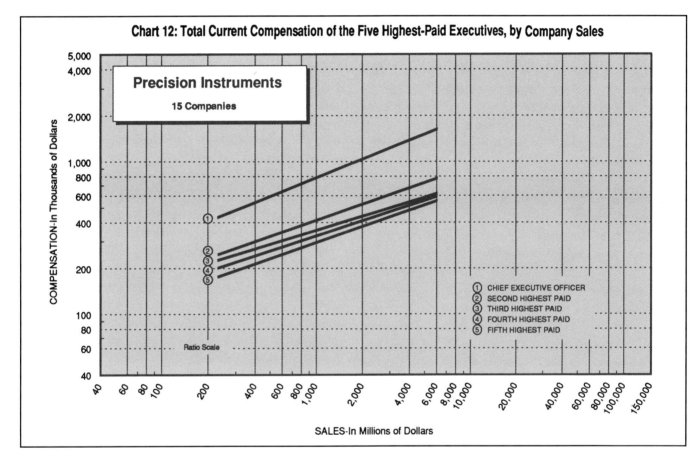

Chart 12: Total Current Compensation of the Five Highest-Paid Executives, by Company Sales

Precision Instruments

15 Companies

COMPENSATION-In Thousands of Dollars

Ratio Scale

① CHIEF EXECUTIVE OFFICER
② SECOND HIGHEST PAID
③ THIRD HIGHEST PAID
④ FOURTH HIGHEST PAID
⑤ FIFTH HIGHEST PAID

SALES-In Millions of Dollars

Table 100: 1990 Sales Volume

1990 Sales	Companies	
	Number	Percent
$5 billion and over	1	7%
2-4,999 billion	1	7
1-1,999 billion	1	7
500-999 million	6	40
300-499 million	2	13
299 million and under	4	27
Total	15	100%

Median	Middle 50% Range	
	Low	High
$598 million	$252 million	$838 million

Table 101: 1990 Total Current Compensation

Compensation Rank	Median	Middle 50% Range	
		Low	High
CEO	$575,000	$353,000	$791,000
Second highest	305,000	260,000	496,000
Third highest	294,000	203,000	420,000
Fourth highest	257,000	180,000	340,000
Fifth highest	207,000	171,000	297,000

Table 102: 1990 Total Current Compensation Regression Formula

Compensation Rank	Formula	r^2
CEO	log Y = 1.6730 + 0.4070 log X	26%
Second highest	log Y = 1.5640 + 0.3500 log X	40
Third highest	log Y = 1.6400 + 0.3020 log X	36
Fourth highest	log Y = 1.5210 + 0.3310 log X	41
Fifth highest	log Y = 1.4250 + 0.3470 log X	42

Table 103: Total Current Compensation as a Percentage of CEO's Total Current Compensation

Compensation Rank	Median	Middle 50% Range	
		Low	High
Second highest	58%	52%	63%
Third highest	51	43	53
Fourth highest	45	40	50
Fifth highest	40	35	46

Table 104: 1990 Salary

Compensation Rank	Median	Middle 50% Range	
		Low	High
CEO	$340,000	$265,000	$485,000
Second highest	225,000	175,000	285,000
Third highest	204,000	148,000	250,000
Fourth highest	170,000	146,000	230,000
Fifth highest	155,000	130,000	200,000

Table 105: 1990 Salary Regression Formula

Compensation Rank	Formula	r^2
CEO	log Y = 1.4780 + 0.4020 log X	65%
Second highest	log Y = 1.4460 + 0.3390 log X	71
Third highest	log Y = 1.4640 + 0.3100 log X	55
Fourth highest	log Y = 1.4290 + 0.3110 log X	60
Fifth highest	log Y = 1.3540 + 0.3180 log X	74

Table 106: Salary as a Percentage of CEO's Salary

Compensation Rank	Median	Middle 50% Range	
		Low	High
Second highest	66%	55%	67%
Third highest	56	45	57
Fourth highest	49	45	59
Fifth highest	46	40	49

Primary Metals (including Steel)

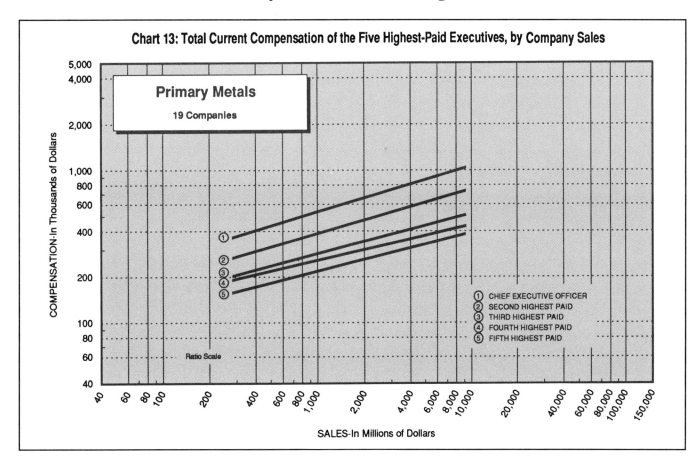

Chart 13: Total Current Compensation of the Five Highest-Paid Executives, by Company Sales

Primary Metals

19 Companies

COMPENSATION-In Thousands of Dollars

① CHIEF EXECUTIVE OFFICER
② SECOND HIGHEST PAID
③ THIRD HIGHEST PAID
④ FOURTH HIGHEST PAID
⑤ FIFTH HIGHEST PAID

Ratio Scale

SALES-In Millions of Dollars

Table 107: 1990 Sales Volume

1990 Sales	Companies	
	Number	Percent
$5 billion and over	1	5%
2-4,999 billion	8	42
1-1,999 billion	4	21
500-999 million	4	21
300-499 million	1	5
299 million and under	1	5
Total	19	100%

Median	Middle 50% Range	
	Low	High
$1.2 billion	$874 million	$2.6 billion

Table 108: 1990 Total Current Compensation

Compensation Rank	Median	Middle 50% Range	
		Low	High
CEO	$613,000	$402,000	$848,000
Second highest	391,000	300,000	617,000
Third highest	351,000	245,000	428,000
Fourth highest	317,000	199,000	410,000
Fifth highest	241,000	176,000	341,000

Table 109: 1990 Total Current Compensation Regression Formula

Compensation Rank	Formula	r^2
CEO	log Y = 1.8010 + 0.3100 log X	38%
Second highest	log Y = 1.6870 + 0.3010 log X	29
Third highest	log Y = 1.6310 + 0.2760 log X	31
Fourth highest	log Y = 1.6810 + 0.2440 log X	28
Fifth highest	log Y = 1.5540 + 0.2630 log X	31

Table 110: Total Current Compensation as a Percentage of CEO's Total Current Compensation

Compensation Rank	Median	Middle 50% Range	
		Low	High
Second highest	73%	64%	81%
Third highest	52	43	65
Fourth highest	44	37	61
Fifth highest	40	30	50

Table 111: 1990 Salary

Compensation Rank	Median	Middle 50% Range	
		Low	High
CEO	$361,000	$241,000	$470,000
Second highest	223,000	162,000	288,000
Third highest	173,000	146,000	306,000
Fourth highest	170,000	132,000	206,000
Fifth highest	143,000	114,000	192,000

Table 112: 1990 Salary Regression Formula

Compensation Rank	Formula	r^2
CEO	log Y = 1.5500 + 0.3290 log X	83%
Second highest	log Y = 1.5370 + 0.2670 log X	77
Third highest	log Y = 1.4450 + 0.2760 log X	45
Fourth highest	log Y = 1.4110 + 0.2690 log X	56
Fifth highest	log Y = 1.3500 + 0.2770 log X	75

Table 113: Salary as a Percentage of CEO's Salary

Compensation Rank	Median	Middle 50% Range	
		Low	High
Second highest	68%	56%	71%
Third highest	53	46	68
Fourth highest	46	41	55
Fifth highest	45	37	52

Transportation Equipment

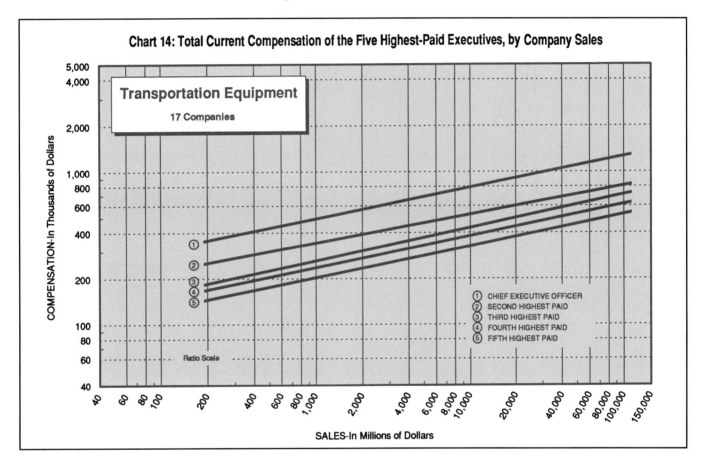

Chart 14: Total Current Compensation of the Five Highest-Paid Executives, by Company Sales

Transportation Equipment
17 Companies

COMPENSATION-In Thousands of Dollars

① CHIEF EXECUTIVE OFFICER
② SECOND HIGHEST PAID
③ THIRD HIGHEST PAID
④ FOURTH HIGHEST PAID
⑤ FIFTH HIGHEST PAID

Ratio Scale

SALES-In Millions of Dollars

Table 114: 1990 Sales Volume

| 1990 Sales | Companies | |
	Number	Percent
$5 billion and over	4	24%
2-4,999 billion	5	29
1-1,999 billion	—	—
500-999 million	4	24
300-499 million	2	12
200-299 million	1	6
199 million and under	1	6
Total	17	100%

| Median | Middle 50% Range | |
	Low	High
$2.6 billion	$694 million	$5 billion

Table 115: 1990 Total Current Compensation

| Compensation Rank | Median | Middle 50% Range | |
		Low	High
CEO	$613,000	$411,000	$935,000
Second highest	404,000	298,000	587,000
Third highest	332,000	202,000	478,000
Fourth highest	296,000	195,000	425,000
Fifth highest	240,000	166,000	381,000

Table 116: 1990 Total Current Compensation Regression Formula

Compensation Rank	Formula	r^2
CEO	log Y = 2.0800 + 0.2040 log X	63%
Second highest	log Y = 1.9670 + 0.1880 log X	65
Third highest	log Y = 1.7690 + 0.2160 log X	70
Fourth highest	log Y = 1.7510 + 0.2070 log X	67
Fifth highest	log Y = 1.6840 + 0.2080 log X	71

Table 117: Total Current Compensation as a Percentage of CEO's Total Current Compensation

Compensation Rank	Median	Middle 50% Range	
		Low	High
Second highest	66%	59%	80%
Third highest	54	50	61
Fourth highest	48	44	55
Fifth highest	40	38	45

Table 118: 1990 Salary

Compensation Rank	Median	Middle 50% Range	
		Low	High
CEO	$475,000	$273,000	$772,000
Second highest	350,000	202,000	535,000
Third highest	235,000	158,000	418,000
Fourth highest	220,000	138,000	365,000
Fifth highest	190,000	127,000	313,000

Table 119: 1990 Salary Regression Formula

Compensation Rank	Formula	r^2
CEO	log Y = 1.9040 + 0.2220 log X	81%
Second highest	log Y = 1.8390 + 0.1950 log X	78
Third highest	log Y = 1.6020 + 0.2280 log X	87
Fourth highest	log Y = 1.5520 + 0.2310 log X	92
Fifth highest	log Y = 1.5710 + 0.2120 log X	93

Table 120: Salary as a Percentage of CEO's Salary

Compensation Rank	Median	Middle 50% Range	
		Low	High
Second highest	75%	56%	83%
Third highest	54	44	62
Fourth highest	48	44	54
Fifth highest	42	39	49

Commercial Banking

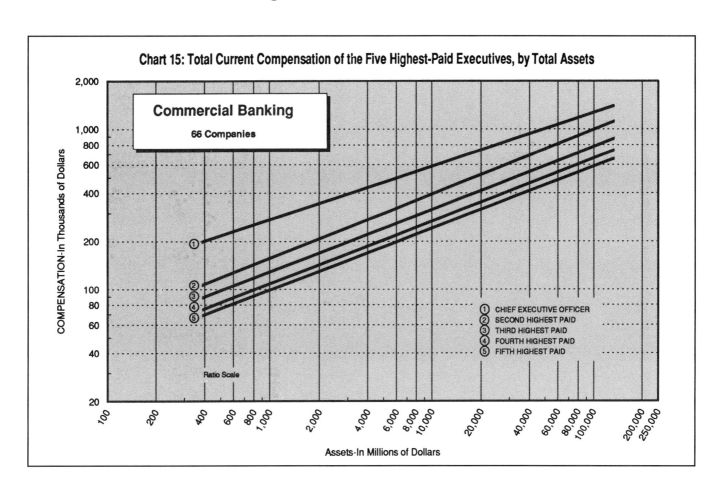

Chart 15: Total Current Compensation of the Five Highest-Paid Executives, by Total Assets

Commercial Banking

66 Companies

COMPENSATION-In Thousands of Dollars

Ratio Scale

① CHIEF EXECUTIVE OFFICER
② SECOND HIGHEST PAID
③ THIRD HIGHEST PAID
④ FOURTH HIGHEST PAID
⑤ FIFTH HIGHEST PAID

Assets-In Millions of Dollars

Table 121: 1990 Total Assets

1990 Total Assets	Companies	
	Number	Percent
$5 billion and over	37	56%
2-4,999 billion	15	23
1-1,999 billion	4	6
500-999 million	9	14
300-499 million	1	2
Total	66	100%

	Middle 50% Range	
Median	Low	High
$6.1 billion	$2.4 billion	$17.5 billion

Table 122: 1990 Total Current Compensation

Compensation Rank	Median	Middle 50% Range	
		Low	High
CEO	$470,000	$324,000	$765,000
Second highest	324,000	208,000	514,000
Third highest	253,000	168,000	421,000
Fourth highest	207,000	132,000	319,000
Fifth highest	187,000	129,000	301,000

Table 123: 1990 Total Current Compensation Regression Formula

Compensation Rank	Formula	r^2
CEO	log Y = 1.4290 + 0.3350 log X	59%
Second highest	log Y = 0.9820 + 0.4030 log X	72
Third highest	log Y = 0.9310 + 0.3920 log X	72
Fourth highest	log Y = 0.8540 + 0.3930 log X	72
Fifth highest	log Y = 0.8360 + 0.3860 log X	74

Table 124: Total Current Compensation as a Percentage of CEO's Total Current Compensation

Compensation Rank	Median	Middle 50% Range	
		Low	High
Second highest	67%	55%	78%
Third highest	52	44	64
Fourth highest	43	37	52
Fifth highest	41	32	48

Table 125: 1990 Salary

Compensation Rank	Median	Middle 50% Range	
		Low	High
CEO	$393,000	$269,000	$555,000
Second highest	268,000	178,000	400,000
Third highest	215,000	148,000	319,000
Fourth highest	180,000	125,000	261,000
Fifth highest	165,000	120,000	236,000

Table 126: 1990 Salary Regression Formula

Compensation Rank	Formula	r^2
CEO	log Y = 1.6100 + 0.2540 log X	48%
Second highest	log Y = 1.1660 + 0.3300 log X	73
Third highest	log Y = 1.1870 + 0.3000 log X	72
Fourth highest	log Y = 1.1090 + 0.3030 log X	75
Fifth highest	log Y = 1.0840 + 0.2990 log X	78

Table 127: Salary as a Percentage of CEO's Salary

Compensation Rank	Median	Middle 50% Range	
		Low	High
Second highest	67%	58%	78%
Third highest	54	46	64
Fourth highest	45	40	55
Fifth highest	42	35	52

Table 128: 1990 Bonus Awards (as Percent of Salary) by Company Size

Executive	Total Assets		
	Middle 50% Range		
	Low $2.4 Billion	Median $6.1 Billion	High $17.5 Billion
CEO			
1990 Bonus	44%	53%	65%
Salary	$294,000	$366,000	$467,000
Second Highest			
1990 Bonus	26%	35%	45%
Salary	$194,000	$258,000	$356,000
Third Highest			
1990 Bonus	24%	35%	49%
Salary	$154,000	$204,000	$280,000
Fourth Highest			
1990 Bonus	21%	33%	46%
Salary	$136,000	$178,000	$243,000
Fifth Highest			
1990 Bonus	20%	30%	43%
Salary	$123,000	$161,000	$219,000

Table 129: 1990 Bonus Awards

1990 Bonus Awards (Percent of Salary)	CEOS		Second Highest Paid		Third Highest Paid		Fourth Highest Paid		Fifth Highest Paid	
	Number	Percent	Number	Percent	Number	Percent	Number	Percent	Number	Percent
100% or more	7	17%	3	8%	3	7%	3	7%	3	7%
70-99	4	10	6	15	4	10	2	5	2	5
60-69	1	2	1	3	4	10	2	5	2	5
50-59	4	10	2	5	—	—	—	—	1	2
40-49	4	10	3	8	5	12	3	7	2	5
30-39	8	19	8	21	6	14	9	21	10	23
20-29	9	21	9	23	10	24	12	27	10	23
Less than 20%	5	12	7	18	10	24	13	30	13	30
Total	42	100%	39	100%	42	100%	44	100%	43	100%
Median Bonus	38%		35%		30%		25%		25%	
Middle 50% Range	25-78%		20-64%		20-63%		17-38%		15-39%	

Communications

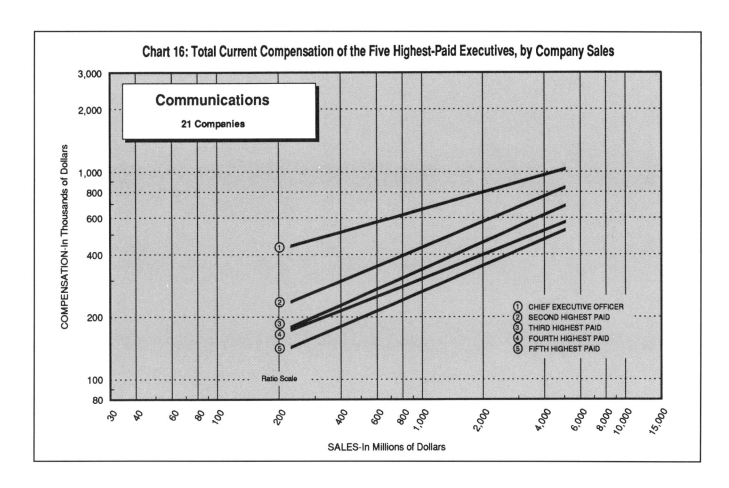

Chart 16: Total Current Compensation of the Five Highest-Paid Executives, by Company Sales

Communications

21 Companies

COMPENSATION-In Thousands of Dollars

Ratio Scale

① CHIEF EXECUTIVE OFFICER
② SECOND HIGHEST PAID
③ THIRD HIGHEST PAID
④ FOURTH HIGHEST PAID
⑤ FIFTH HIGHEST PAID

SALES-In Millions of Dollars

Table 130: 1990 Sales Volume

1990 Sales Volume	Companies	
	Number	Percent
$2 billion and over	5	24%
1-1,999 billion	5	24
500-999 million	5	24
300-499 million	5	24
299 million and under	1	5
Total	21	100%

Median	Middle 50% Range	
	Low	High
$812 million	$439 million	$1.8 billion

Table 131: 1990 Total Current Compensation

Compensation Rank	Median	Middle 50% Range	
		Low	High
CEO	$630,000	$485,000	$884,000
Second highest	435,000	285,000	588,000
Third highest	362,000	237,000	474,000
Fourth highest	299,000	225,000	467,000
Fifth highest	273,000	197,000	364,000

Table 132: 1990 Total Current Compensation Regression Formula

Compensation Rank	Formula	r^2
CEO	log Y = 1.9960 + 0.2740 log X	37%
Second highest	log Y = 1.4130 + 0.4080 log X	47
Third highest	log Y = 1.2110 + 0.4390 log X	50
Fourth highest	log Y = 1.3380 + 0.3830 log X	46
Fifth highest	log Y = 1.1620 + 0.4200 log X	58

Table 133: Total Current Compensation as a Percentage of CEO's Total Current Compensation

Compensation Rank	Median	Middle 50% Range Low	Middle 50% Range High
Second highest	71%	55%	87%
Third highest	50	43	73
Fourth highest	43	37	66
Fifth highest	38	33	54

Table 134: 1990 Salary

Compensation Rank	Median	Middle 50% Range Low	Middle 50% Range High
CEO	$480,000	$410,000	$650,000
Second highest	380,000	201,000	535,000
Third highest	274,000	200,000	400,000
Fourth highest	282,000	175,000	330,000
Fifth highest	243,000	175,000	300,000

Table 135: 1990 Salary Regression Formula

Compensation Rank	Formula	r^2
CEO	log Y = 2.2620 + 0.1390 log X	18%
Second highest	log Y = 1.6780 + 0.2760 log X	30
Third highest	log Y = 1.8680 + 0.1860 log X	20
Fourth highest	log Y = 1.9420 + 0.1500 log X	14
Fifth highest	log Y = 1.6310 + 0.2320 log X	32

Table 136: Salary as a Percentage of CEO's Salary

Compensation Rank	Median	Middle 50% Range Low	Middle 50% Range High
Second highest	75%	61%	82%
Third highest	58	44	70
Fourth highest	52	39	65
Fifth highest	39	37	61

Table 137: 1990 Bonus Awards (as Percent of Salary) by Company Size

Executive	Sales Volume Middle 50% Range Low $439 Million	Sales Volume Middle 50% Range Median $812 Million	Sales Volume Middle 50% Range High $1.8 Billion
CEO			
1990 Bonus	35%	41%	49%
Salary	$426,000	$464,000	$518,000
Second Highest			
1990 Bonus	24%	32%	42%
Salary	$256,000	$303,000	$377,000
Third Highest			
1990 Bonus	27%	36%	49%
Salary	$229,000	$257,000	$298,000
Fourth Highest			
1990 Bonus	25%	34%	45%
Salary	$218,000	$239,000	$269,000
Fifth Highest			
1990 Bonus	18%	27%	40%
Salary	$175,000	$202,000	$243,000

Diversified Services

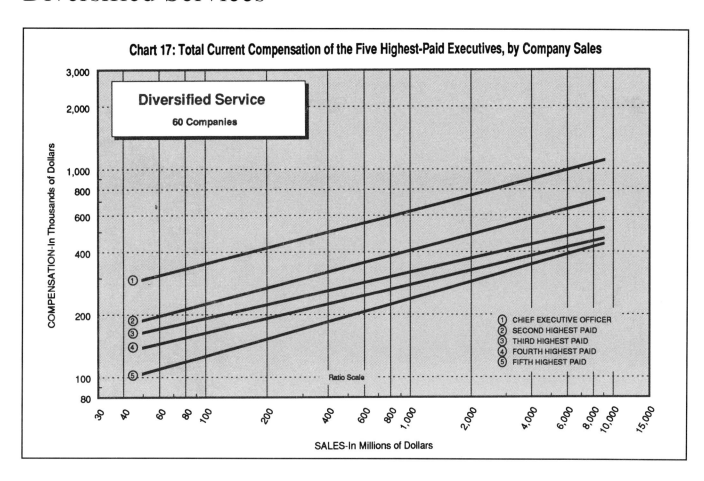

Chart 17: Total Current Compensation of the Five Highest-Paid Executives, by Company Sales

Diversified Service
60 Companies

COMPENSATION-In Thousands of Dollars

① CHIEF EXECUTIVE OFFICER
② SECOND HIGHEST PAID
③ THIRD HIGHEST PAID
④ FOURTH HIGHEST PAID
⑤ FIFTH HIGHEST PAID

Ratio Scale

SALES-In Millions of Dollars

Table 138: 1990 Sales Volume

1990 Sales Volume	Companies	
	Number	Percent
$5 billion and over	6	10%
2-4,999 billion	5	8
1-1,999 billion	16	27
500-999 million	11	18
300-499 million	9	15
200-299 million	6	10
199 million and under	7	12
Total	60	100%

Median	Middle 50% Range	
	Low	High
$850 million	$307 million	$1.7 billion

Table 139: 1990 Total Current Compensation

Compensation Rank	Median	Middle 50% Range	
		Low	High
CEO	$666,000	$393,000	$816,000
Second highest	397,000	219,000	570,000
Third highest	309,000	190,000	492,000
Fourth highest	250,000	166,000	392,000
Fifth highest	221,000	152,000	384,000

Table 140: 1990 Total Current Compensation Regression Formula

Compensation Rank	Formula	r^2
CEO	log Y = 2.0310 + 0.2590 log X	30%
Second highest	log Y = 1.8300 + 0.2620 log X	31
Third highest	log Y = 1.8250 + 0.2290 log X	29
Fourth highest	log Y = 1.7390 + 0.2370 log X	32
Fifth highest	log Y = 1.5380 + 0.2820 log X	39

Table 141: Total Current Compensation as a Percentage of CEO's Total Current Compensation

Compensation Rank	Median	Middle 50% Range Low	Middle 50% Range High
Second highest	68%	53%	82%
Third highest	50	40	63
Fourth highest	44	35	53
Fifth highest	38	28	48

Table 142: 1990 Salary

Compensation Rank	Median	Middle 50% Range Low	Middle 50% Range High
CEO	$435,000	$270,000	$645,000
Second highest	265,000	184,000	447,000
Third highest	200,000	165,000	305,000
Fourth highest	196,000	141,000	281,000
Fifth highest	178,000	125,000	264,000

Table 143: 1990 Salary Regression Formula

Compensation Rank	Formula	r^2
CEO	log Y = 1.7540 + 0.2940 log X	45%
Second highest	log Y = 1.6950 + 0.2550 log X	34
Third highest	log Y = 1.6450 + 0.2390 log X	47
Fourth highest	log Y = 1.5940 + 0.2390 log X	40
Fifth highest	log Y = 1.5270 + 0.2500 log X	47

Table 144: Salary as a Percentage of CEO's Salary

Compensation Rank	Median	Middle 50% Range Low	Middle 50% Range High
Second highest	69%	52%	84%
Third highest	54	45	63
Fourth highest	49	40	59
Fifth highest	44	36	58

Table 145: 1990 Bonus Awards (as Percent of Salary) by Company Size

Executive	Sales Volume Middle 50% Range Low $307 Million	Sales Volume Middle 50% Range Median $850 Billion	Sales Volume Middle 50% Range High $1.7 Billion
CEO			
1990 Bonus	69%	62%	58%
Salary	$298,000	$408,000	$504,000
Second Highest			
1990 Bonus	52%	53%	54%
Salary	$213,000	$274,000	$325,000
Third Highest			
1990 Bonus	53%	50%	49%
Salary	$174,000	$226,000	$269,000
Fourth Highest			
1990 Bonus	46%	46%	45%
Salary	$156,000	$200,000	$238,000
Fifth Highest			
1990 Bonus	30%	36%	39%
Salary	$142,000	$184,000	$220,000

Table 146: 1990 Bonus Awards

1990 Bonus Awards (Percent of Salary)	CEOs Number	CEOs Percent	Second Highest Paid Number	Second Highest Paid Percent	Third Highest Paid Number	Third Highest Paid Percent	Fourth Highest Paid Number	Fourth Highest Paid Percent	Fifth Highest Paid Number	Fifth Highest Paid Percent
100% or more	7	15%	6	13%	6	14%	4	9%	3	7%
70-99	13	28	11	24	9	21	7	16	4	10
60-69	3	6	3	7	3	7	2	5	2	5
50-59	7	15	1	2	4	9	5	11	4	10
40-49	3	6	4	9	3	7	7	16	7	17
30-39	4	9	11	24	6	14	4	9	5	12
20-29	6	13	5	11	7	16	7	16	5	12
Less than 20%	4	9	4	9	5	12	8	18	11	27
Total	47	100%	45	100%	43	100%	44	100%	41	100%
Median Bonus	58%		46%		50%		44%		38%	
Middle 50% Range	32-87%		31-81%		26-79%		25-64%		19-57%	

Energy and Natural Resources

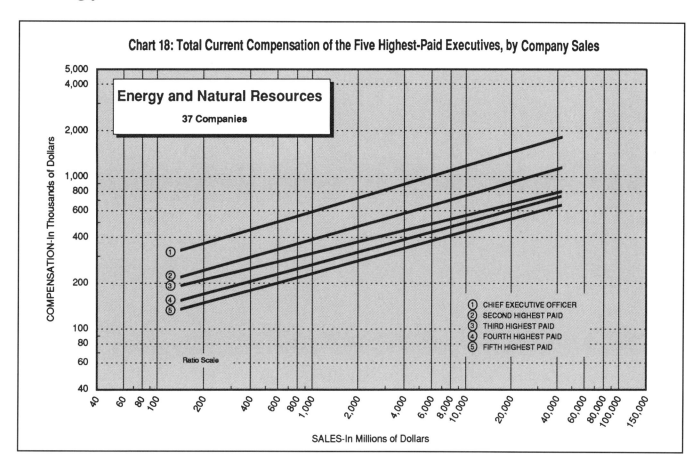

Chart 18: Total Current Compensation of the Five Highest-Paid Executives, by Company Sales

Energy and Natural Resources

37 Companies

COMPENSATION-In Thousands of Dollars

Ratio Scale

① CHIEF EXECUTIVE OFFICER
② SECOND HIGHEST PAID
③ THIRD HIGHEST PAID
④ FOURTH HIGHEST PAID
⑤ FIFTH HIGHEST PAID

SALES-In Millions of Dollars

Table 147: 1990 Sales Volume

1990 Sales	Companies	
	Number	Percent
$5 billion and over	12	32%
2-4,999 billion	12	32
1-1,999 billion	2	5
500-999 million	7	19
300-499 million	2	5
200-299 million	—	—
199 million and under	2	5
Total	37	100%

Median	Middle 50% Range	
	Low	High
$2.3 billion	$874 million	$11.8 billion

Table 148: 1990 Total Current Compensation

Compensation Rank	Median	Middle 50% Range	
		Low	High
CEO	$809,000	$548,000	$1,263,000
Second highest	520,000	342,000	810,000
Third highest	354,000	278,000	519,000
Fourth highest	329,000	236,000	503,000
Fifth highest	300,000	194,000	468,000

Table 149: 1990 Total Current Compensation Regression Formula

Compensation Rank	Formula	r^2
CEO	$\log Y = 1.8730 + 0.3000 \log X$	71%
Second highest	$\log Y = 1.7140 + 0.2910 \log X$	62
Third highest	$\log Y = 1.7470 + 0.2500 \log X$	59
Fourth highest	$\log Y = 1.5950 + 0.2760 \log X$	65
Fifth highest	$\log Y = 1.5290 + 0.2780 \log X$	64

Table 150: Total Current Compensation as a Percentage of CEO's Total Current Compensation

Compensation Rank	Median	Middle 50% Range	
		Low	High
Second highest	67%	57%	75%
Third highest	51	41	60
Fourth highest	44	37	54
Fifth highest	38	33	45

Table 151: 1990 Salary

Compensation Rank	Median	Middle 50% Range	
		Low	High
CEO	$520,000	$410,000	$668,000
Second highest	325,000	276,000	432,000
Third highest	279,000	220,000	332,000
Fourth highest	220,000	185,000	328,000
Fifth highest	190,000	170,000	272,000

Table 152: 1990 Salary Regression Formula

Compensation Rank	Formula	r^2
CEO	$\log Y = 2.0600 + 0.1890 \log X$	73%
Second highest	$\log Y = 1.8450 + 0.1940 \log X$	50
Third highest	$\log Y = 1.9350 + 0.1420 \log X$	40
Fourth highest	$\log Y = 1.6760 + 0.2050 \log X$	61
Fifth highest	$\log Y = 1.6780 + 0.1830 \log X$	52

Table 153: Salary as a Percentage of CEO's Salary

Compensation Rank	Median	Middle 50% Range	
		Low	High
Second highest	63%	56%	76%
Third highest	51	45	60
Fourth highest	46	39	52
Fifth highest	42	37	46

Table 154: 1990 Bonus Awards (as Percent of Salary) by Company Size

Executive	Sales Volume		
	Middle 50% Range		
	Low $874 Million	Median $2.3 Billion	High $11.8 Billion
CEO			
1990 Bonus	46%	55%	71%
Salary	$414,000	$496,000	$675,000
Second Highest			
1990 Bonus	45%	53%	65%
Salary	$260,000	$314,000	$432,000
Third Highest			
1990 Bonus	38%	47%	64%
Salary	$225,000	$258,000	$326,000
Fourth Highest			
1990 Bonus	38%	41%	48%
Salary	$190,000	$232,000	$324,000
Fifth Highest			
1990 Bonus	36%	45%	59%
Salary	$165,000	$196,000	$265,000

Table 155: 1990 Bonus Awards

1990 Bonus Awards (Percent of Salary)	CEOs		Second Highest Paid		Third Highest Paid		Fourth Highest Paid		Fifth Highest Paid	
	Number	Percent	Number	Percent	Number	Percent	Number	Percent	Number	Percent
100% or more	3	12%	1	4%	2	8%	1	4%	1	4%
70-99	7	28	6	22	5	19	2	8	3	12
40-69	9	36	12	44	9	35	11	44	11	42
20-39	4	16	6	22	6	23	8	32	8	31
Less than 20%	2	8	2	7	4	15	3	12	3	12
Total	25	100%	27	100%	26	100%	25	100%	26	100%
Median Bonus	64%		56%		47%		47%		49%	
Middle 50% Range	40-79%		28-70%		27-75%		28-60%		24-62%	

Insurance

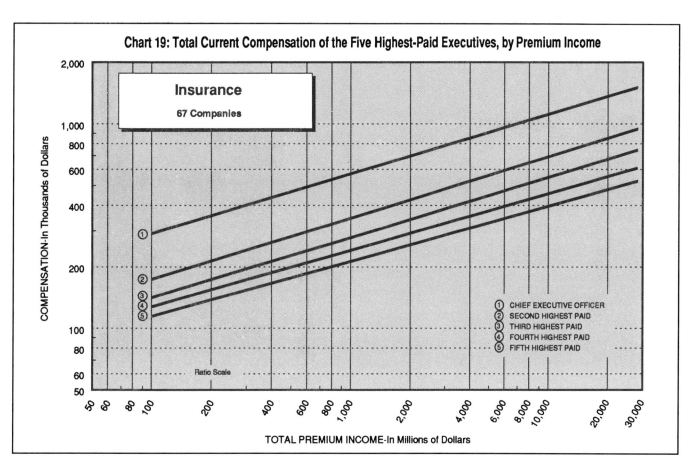

Chart 19: Total Current Compensation of the Five Highest-Paid Executives, by Premium Income

Insurance
67 Companies

COMPENSATION-In Thousands of Dollars

① CHIEF EXECUTIVE OFFICER
② SECOND HIGHEST PAID
③ THIRD HIGHEST PAID
④ FOURTH HIGHEST PAID
⑤ FIFTH HIGHEST PAID

Ratio Scale

TOTAL PREMIUM INCOME-In Millions of Dollars

Table 156: 1990 Premium Income

1990 Premium Income	Companies Number	Companies Percent
$5 billion and over	12	18%
2-4,999 billion	8	12
1-1,999 billion	8	12
500-999 million	11	16
300-499 million	7	10
200-299 million	7	10
199 million and under	14	21
Total	67	100%

Median	Middle 50% Range Low	Middle 50% Range High
$578 million	$232 million	$3.3 billion

Table 157: 1990 Total Current Compensation

Compensation Rank	Median	Middle 50% Range Low	Middle 50% Range High
CEO	$533,000	$332,000	$945,000
Second highest	331,000	199,000	533,000
Third highest	260,000	154,000	455,000
Fourth highest	222,000	138,000	415,000
Fifth highest	200,000	122,000	342,000

Table 158: 1990 Total Current Compensation Regression

Compensation Rank	Formula	r^2
CEO	log Y = 1.8610+ 0.2960 log X	55%
Second highest	log Y = 1.6230 + 0.3040 log X	60
Third highest	log Y = 1.5410 + 0.2990 log X	59
Fourth highest	log Y = 1.5360 + 0.2800 log X	58
Fifth highest	log Y = 1.5050 + 0.2730 log X	59

Table 159: Total Current Compensation as a Percentage of CEO's Total Current Compensation

Compensation Rank	Median	Middle 50% Range Low	Middle 50% Range High
Second highest	61%	52%	74%
Third highest	49	43	57
Fourth highest	42	36	48
Fifth highest	38	33	44

Table 160: 1990 Salary

Compensation Rank	Median	Middle 50% Range Low	Middle 50% Range High
CEO	$390,000	$270,000	$613,000
Second highest	250,000	171,000	365,000
Third highest	200,000	138,000	310,000
Fourth highest	168,000	118,000	262,000
Fifth highest	148,000	105,000	242,000

Table 161: 1990 Salary Regression Formula

Compensation Rank	Formula	r^2
CEO	log Y = 1.8550 + 0.2530 log X	65%
Second highest	log Y = 1.6370 + 0.2600 log X	64
Third highest	log Y = 1.5650 + 0.2550 log X	61
Fourth highest	log Y = 1.5420 + 0.2440 log X	66
Fifth highest	log Y = 1.5100 + 0.2390 log X	68

Table 162: Salary as a Percentage of CEO's Salary

Compensation Rank	Median	Middle 50% Range Low	Middle 50% Range High
Second highest	65%	56%	74%
Third highest	51	46	61
Fourth highest	45	40	53
Fifth highest	41	35	48

Table 163: 1990 Bonus Awards (as Percent of Salary) by Company Size

Executive	Premium Income Middle 50% Range Low $232 Million	Premium Income Middle 50% Range Median $578 Million	Premium Income Middle 50% Range High $3.3 Billion
CEO			
1990 Bonus	40%	44%	53%
Salary	$309,000	$373,000	$535,000
Second Highest			
1990 Bonus	32%	36%	46%
Salary	$190,000	$233,000	$342,000
Third Highest			
1990 Bonus	28%	33%	42%
Salary	$158,000	$191,000	$276,000
Fourth Highest			
1990 Bonus	27%	31%	39%
Salary	$139,000	$169,000	$246,000
Fifth Highest			
1990 Bonus	25%	29%	35%
Salary	$127,000	$154,000	$224,000

Table 164: 1990 Bonus Awards

1990 Bonus Awards (Percent of Salary)	CEOS Number	CEOS Percent	Second Highest Paid Number	Second Highest Paid Percent	Third Highest Paid Number	Third Highest Paid Percent	Fourth Highest Paid Number	Fourth Highest Paid Percent	Fifth Highest Paid Number	Fifth Highest Paid Percent
70% or more	14	26%	10	19%	6	11%	6	11%	6	11%
60-69	1	2	4	8	6	11	3	6	2	4
50-59	6	11	3	6	5	9	3	6	5	9
40-49	7	13	7	13	5	9	3	6	3	6
30-39	11	20	12	23	6	11	13	24	11	21
20-29	7	13	9	17	16	30	15	28	13	25
10-19	3	6	4	8	5	9	5	9	6	11
Less than 10%	5	9	4	8	4	8	6	11	7	13
Total	54	100%	53	100%	53	100%	54	100%	53	100%
Median Bonus	40%		34%		31%		30%		30%	
Middle 50% Range	28-72%		25-60%		23-58%		21-46%		21-48%	

Life Insurance

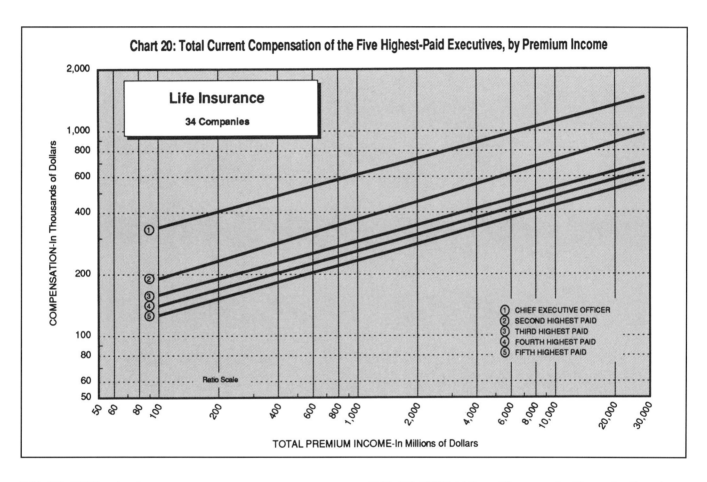

Chart 20: Total Current Compensation of the Five Highest-Paid Executives, by Premium Income

Life Insurance

34 Companies

COMPENSATION-In Thousands of Dollars

① CHIEF EXECUTIVE OFFICER
② SECOND HIGHEST PAID
③ THIRD HIGHEST PAID
④ FOURTH HIGHEST PAID
⑤ FIFTH HIGHEST PAID

Ratio Scale

TOTAL PREMIUM INCOME-In Millions of Dollars

Table 165: 1990 Premium Income

1990 Premium Income	Companies Number	Percent
$5 billion and over	6	18%
2-4,999 billion	3	9
1-1,999 billion	4	12
500-999 million	6	18
300-499 million	3	9
200-299 million	3	9
199 million and under	9	27
Total	34	100%

| Median | Middle 50% Range | |
	Low	High
$539 million	$174 million	$3.2 billion

Table 166: 1990 Total Current Compensation Regression Formula

Compensation Rank	Formula	r^2
CEO	$\log Y = 1.9960 + 0.2620 \log X$	46%
Second highest	$\log Y = 1.6900 + 0.2910 \log X$	56
Third highest	$\log Y = 1.6630 + 0.2650 \log X$	49
Fourth highest	$\log Y = 1.5960 + 0.2710 \log X$	49
Fifth highest	$\log Y = 1.5520 + 0.2710 \log X$	55

SUB: TEC FILE: t159-166 pg2

Table 167: 1990 Salary Regression Formula

Compensation Rank	Formula	r^2
CEO	$\log Y = 1.9600 + 0.2270 \log X$	64%
Second highest	$\log Y = 1.6960 + 0.2470 \log X$	66
Third highest	$\log Y = 1.6880 + 0.2180 \log X$	55
Fourth highest	$\log Y = 1.6050 + 0.2320 \log X$	59
Fifth highest	$\log Y = 1.5940 + 0.2200 \log X$	61

Property and Casualty Insurance

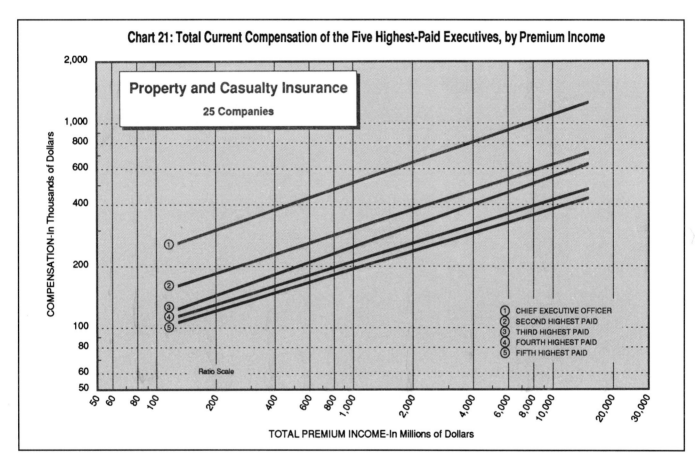

Chart 21: Total Current Compensation of the Five Highest-Paid Executives, by Premium Income

Property and Casualty Insurance

25 Companies

COMPENSATION-In Thousands of Dollars

① CHIEF EXECUTIVE OFFICER
② SECOND HIGHEST PAID
③ THIRD HIGHEST PAID
④ FOURTH HIGHEST PAID
⑤ FIFTH HIGHEST PAID

Ratio Scale

TOTAL PREMIUM INCOME-In Millions of Dollars

Table 168: 1990 Premium Income

	Companies	
1990 Premium Income	Number	Percent
$5 billion and over	6	24%
2-4,999 billion	3	12
1-1,999 billion	3	12
500-999 million	4	16
300-499 million	2	8
200-299 million	3	12
199 million and under	4	16
Total	25	100%

	Middle 50% Range	
Median	Low	High
$949 million	$299 million	$4.6 billion

Table 169: 1990 Total Current Compensation Regression Formula

Compensation Rank	Formula	r^2
CEO	log Y = 1.7150 + 0.3320 log X	72%
Second highest	log Y = 1.5480 + 0.3130 log X	70
Third highest	log Y = 1.3720 + 0.3420 log X	77
Fourth highest	log Y = 1.4290 + 0.2990 log X	78
Fifth highest	log Y = 1.4070 + 0.2940 log X	78

Table 170: 1990 Salary Regression Formula

Compensation Rank	Formula	r^2
CEO	log Y = 1.6940+ 0.2970 log X	74%
Second highest	log Y = 1.5150 + 0.2890 log X	67
Third highest	log Y = 1.3450 + 0.3180 log X	74
Fourth highest	log Y = 1.3840 + 0.2840 log X	82
Fifth highest	log Y = 1.3560 + 0.2810 log X	83

Trade

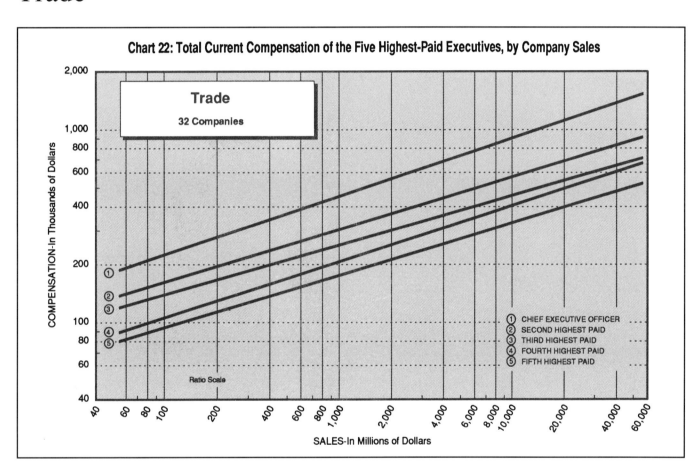

Chart 22: Total Current Compensation of the Five Highest-Paid Executives, by Company Sales

Trade

32 Companies

COMPENSATION-In Thousands of Dollars

① CHIEF EXECUTIVE OFFICER
② SECOND HIGHEST PAID
③ THIRD HIGHEST PAID
④ FOURTH HIGHEST PAID
⑤ FIFTH HIGHEST PAID

Ratio Scale

SALES-In Millions of Dollars

Table 171: 1990 Sales Volume

1990 Sales	Companies Number	Companies Percent
$5 billion and over	11	34%
2-4,999 billion	4	13
1-1,999 billion	5	16
500-999 million	5	16
300-499 million	2	6
200-299 million	1	3
199 million and under	4	13
Total	32	100%

Median	Middle 50% Range Low	Middle 50% Range High
$1.7 billion	$516 million	$7.8 billion

Table 172: 1990 Total Current Compensation

Compensation Rank	Median	Middle 50% Range Low	Middle 50% Range High
CEO	$512,000	$370,000	$983,000
Second highest	326,000	239,000	621,000
Third highest	265,000	209,000	508,000
Fourth highest	226,000	190,000	423,000
Fifth highest	206,000	145,000	347,000

Table 173: 1990 Total Current Compensation Regression Formula

Compensation Rank	Formula	r^2
CEO	log Y = 1.7470 + 0.3030 log X	70%
Second highest	log Y = 1.6650 + 0.2730 log X	66
Third highest	log Y = 1.6290 + 0.2580 log X	66
Fourth highest	log Y = 1.4420 + 0.2920 log X	73
Fifth highest	log Y = 1.4320 + 0.2720 log X	66

Table 174: Total Current Compensation as a Percentage of CEO's Total Current Compensation

Compensation Rank	Median	Middle 50% Range Low	High
Second highest	69%	54%	79%
Third highest	54	44	65
Fourth highest	46	37	54
Fifth highest	39	30	46

Table 175: 1990 Salary

Compensation Rank	Median	Middle 50% Range Low	High
CEO	$425,000	$315,000	$590,000
Second highest	274,000	188,000	400,000
Third highest	213,000	150,000	323,000
Fourth highest	203,000	150,000	307,000
Fifth highest	173,000	131,000	245,000

Table 176: 1990 Salary Regression Formula

Compensation Rank	Formula	r^2
CEO	log Y = 1.8270 + 0.2400 log X	67%
Second highest	log Y = 1.6350 + 0.2450 log X	57
Third highest	log Y = 1.6420 + 0.2210 log X	61
Fourth highest	log Y = 1.4120 + 0.2690 log X	71
Fifth highest	log Y = 1.4620 + 0.2370 log X	64

Table 177: Salary as a Percentage of CEO's Salary

Compensation Rank	Median	Middle 50% Range Low	High
Second highest	67%	57%	81%
Third highest	57	48	67
Fourth highest	50	43	56
Fifth highest	43	35	50

Table 178: 1990 Bonus Awards (as Percent of Salary), by Company Size

Executive	Sales Volume Low $516 Million	Middle 50% Range Median $1.7 Billion	High $7.8 Billion
CEO			
1990 Bonus	31%	40%	53%
Salary	$313,000	$410,000	$579,000
Second Highest			
1990 Bonus	39%	42%	44%
Salary	$196,000	$262,000	$380,000
Third Highest			
1990 Bonus	31%	35%	40%
Salary	$172,000	$223,000	$310,000
Fourth Highest			
1990 Bonus	31%	33%	36%
Salary	$141,000	$192,000	$286,000
Fifth Highest			
1990 Bonus	19%	25%	31%
Salary	$134,000	$173,000	$241,000

Table 179: 1990 Bonus Awards

1990 Bonus Awards (Percent of Salary)	CEOS Number	Percent	Second Highest Paid Number	Percent	Third Highest Paid Number	Percent	Fourth Highest Paid Number	Percent	Fifth Highest Paid Number	Percent
100% or more	1	4%	2	8%	—	—	—	—	—	—
70-99	6	26	5	21	3	12%	3	12%	2	9%
50-69	6	26	3	13	6	24	5	20	2	9
40-49	2	9	2	8	4	16	2	8	3	14
30-39	1	4	2	8	2	8	4	16	3	14
20-29	3	13	5	21	3	12	4	16	1	5
Less than 20%	4	17	5	21	7	28	7	28	11	50
Total	23	100%	24	100%	25	100%	25	100%	22	100%
Median Bonus	55%		35%		40%		34%		18%	
Middle 50% Range	23-71%		21-70%		18-60%		18-50%		15-44%	

Utilities

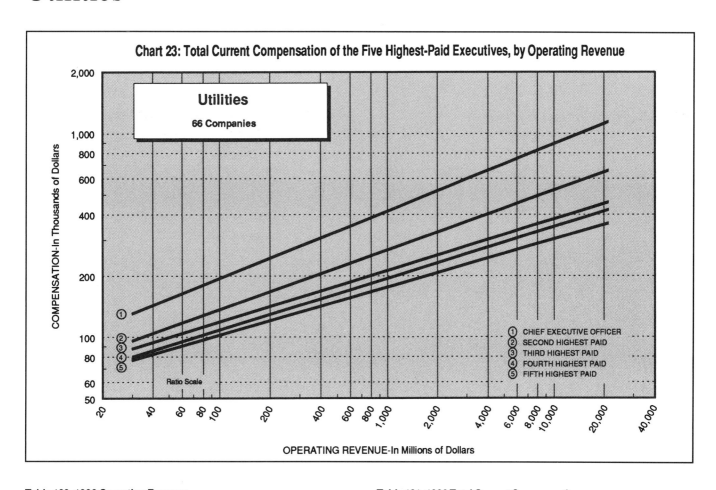

Chart 23: Total Current Compensation of the Five Highest-Paid Executives, by Operating Revenue

Utilities
66 Companies

COMPENSATION-In Thousands of Dollars

Ratio Scale

① CHIEF EXECUTIVE OFFICER
② SECOND HIGHEST PAID
③ THIRD HIGHEST PAID
④ FOURTH HIGHEST PAID
⑤ FIFTH HIGHEST PAID

OPERATING REVENUE-In Millions of Dollars

Table 180: 1990 Operating Revenue

1990 Operating Revenue	Companies	
	Number	Percent
$5 billion and over	10	15%
2-4,999 billion	15	23
1-1,999 billion	12	18
500-999 million	10	15
300-499 million	10	15
200-299 million	3	5
199 million and under	6	9
Total	66	100%

Median	Middle 50% Range	
	Low	High
$1.2 billion	$471 million	$3 billion

Table 181: 1990 Total Current Compensation

Compensation Rank	Median	Middle 50% Range	
		Low	High
CEO	$458,000	$305,000	$599,000
Second highest	271,000	199,000	363,000
Third highest	224,000	160,000	301,000
Fourth highest	200,000	142,000	256,000
Fifth highest	183,000	134,000	232,000

Table 182: 1990 Total Current Compensation Regression Formula

Compensation Rank	Formula	r^2
CEO	log Y = 1.6270 + 0.3310 log X	59%
Second highest	log Y = 1.5480 + 0.2930 log X	49
Third highest	log Y = 1.5720 + 0.2520 log X	46
Fourth highest	log Y = 1.5170 + 0.2560 log X	49
Fifth highest	log Y = 1.5380 + 0.2360 log X	45

Table 183: Total Current Compensation as a Percentage of CEO's Total Current Compensation

Compensation Rank	Median	Middle 50% Range Low	High
Second highest	64%	56%	73%
Third highest	51	43	57
Fourth highest	44	39	51
Fifth highest	42	35	47

Table 184: 1990 Salary

Compensation Rank	Median	Middle 50% Range Low	High
CEO	$373,000	$273,000	$486,000
Second highest	216,000	184,000	307,000
Third highest	182,000	145,000	233,000
Fourth highest	172,000	131,000	210,000
Fifth highest	161,000	127,000	194,000

Table 185: 1990 Salary Regression Formula

Compensation Rank	Formula	r^2
CEO	log Y = 1.7790 + 0.2520 log X	52%
Second highest	log Y = 1.6470 + 0.2350 log X	49
Third highest	log Y = 1.6600 + 0.1980 log X	46
Fourth highest	log Y = 1.6050 + 0.2020 log X	50
Fifth highest	log Y = 1.6290 + 0.1830 log X	44

Table 186: Salary as a Percentage of CEO's Salary

Compensation Rank	Median	Middle 50% Range Low	High
Second highest	65%	59%	74%
Third highest	51	46	59
Fourth highest	46	42	53
Fifth highest	43	38	50

Table 187: 1990 Bonus Awards (as Percent of Salary) by Company Size

Executive	Operating Revenue Middle 50% Range Low $471 Million	Median $1.2 Billion	High $3.0 Billion
CEO			
1990 Bonus	21%	30%	39%
Salary	$286,000	$363,000	$460,000
Second Highest			
1990 Bonus	21%	27%	33%
Salary	$189,000	$238,000	$299,000
Third Highest			
1990 Bonus	21%	26%	31%
Salary	$153,000	$187,000	$227,000
Fourth Highest			
1990 Bonus	21%	26%	32%
Salary	$140,000	$171,000	$208,000
Fifth Highest			
1990 Bonus	18%	24%	29%
Salary	$132,000	$158,000	$190,000

Table 188: 1990 Bonus Awards

1990 Bonus Awards (Percent of Salary)	CEOS Number	Percent	Second Highest Paid Number	Percent	Third Highest Paid Number	Percent	Fourth Highest Paid Number	Percent	Fifth Highest Paid Number	Percent
100% or more	3	7%	2	4%	—	—	—	—	—	—
80-99	3	7	2	4	—	—	1	2%	2	4%
60-79	3	7	—	—	6	13%	4	9	—	—
50-59	2	5	4	8	2	4	2	4	1	2
40-49	6	14	2	4	3	6	3	6	8	18
30-39	10	23	12	27	7	15	10	21	7	16
20-29	5	11	8	18	14	30	9	19	9	20
10-19	8	18	13	29	12	26	14	30	13	29
Less than 10%	4	9	2	4	3	6	4	9	5	11
Total	44	100%	45	100%	47	100%	47	100%	45	100%
Median Bonus	32%		29%		24%		24%		25%	
Middle 50% Range	19-48%		17-38%		16-37%		16-35%		16-38%	